how to survive work

Catholic Sc

A guide for teachers and support staff

CONTENTS

FOREWORD

During his apostolic visit to the United Kingdom in 2010, Benedict XVI met with teachers and pupils from Catholic schools throughout our country in St Mary's University College, Twickenham. He reminded us that there is a distinctive Catholic focus to education:

> In your Catholic schools, there is always a bigger picture over and above the individual subjects you study, the different skills you learn. All the work you do is placed in the context of growing in friendship with God, and all that flows from that friendship. So you learn not just to be good students, but good citizens, good people... Always remember that every subject you study is part of a bigger picture... A good school provides a rounded education for the whole person. And a good Catholic school, over and above this, should help all its students to become saints.

This focus is what marks our Catholic schools out from among the many other schools in our country. Our society, like the Church, has a vested interest in the education of its younger members, and parents, Catholic or not, who have chosen to send their children to a Catholic school have made a wise choice; this is because our schools offer something distinctive – the call "to become saints", not just in heaven but here on earth.

As Christians, this call invites us to live in communion with God and with one another in the family of the Church. In the sacrament of baptism, we were consecrated to share in Jesus' prophetic mission by proclaiming the Good News of the kingdom of God, priestly mission by offering our lives in worship of God, and kingly mission by serving our brothers and sisters. That calling is confirmed in the sacrament of confirmation, when we are sealed with the gift of the Holy Spirit, and celebrated in the sacrament of the Eucharist, when we gather around the altar to be challenged by the word of God and comforted by our devout reception of the Body and Blood of Christ. We offer all that we are and ask that it be transformed so that we may become one body, one spirit in Christ; that is how we become saints.

If that is true of our parishes, then it is also true of our schools, which form an indisputable and essential part of the life of our parishes up and down the country. Our schools, like the parishes which they serve, are families, in which everyone is treated with utmost respect, regardless of their background or academic ability, and helped to grow and develop so that their God-given potential can be fully realised and expressed.

Children spend an awful lot of time in school. Some find it hard, others easy. For many of our children, their school is the only place where they find happiness, peace and stability. In obedience to Christ, who came so that we "may have life, and have it to the full" (John 10:10), we have a duty to do what is right by them all, and to help parents to bring their children up in the practice of the Catholic faith by loving God and their neighbour.

This book will help its readers to understand how they can help the children in our schools to become saints – not least by setting them a good example themselves since, as St Peter says, "Never be a dictator over any group that is put in your charge, but be an example that the whole flock can follow" (1 Peter 5:3). Whether a school is maintained or independent, an academy – conversion or transformational – free school or voluntary aided, it is focused on helping those entrusted to it by their parents to become saints, and this book will help people to understand how that is expressed in the daily lives of our schools.

This focus is expressed in our schools' "Catholic ethos". The ethos is not something that is ancillary to the other aspects of a school's life, but is their foundation stone: every aspect of the school's life must be rooted in its ethos, from the curriculum to the playground, from the staffing structure to school policies. You can read in Chapter 3 about how our schools consistently surpass other schools in national averages, and do so by attracting pupils from a much wider range than do other schools. This is because our schools' ethos – and its concrete expression in celebrations of Mass, assemblies, the commitment of staff and the teaching of religious education – is fundamental to our schools, giving them true and lasting value. As it says in Chapter 5, "Far from diluting academic teaching, the Catholic ethos and sense of purpose should make teaching truly three-dimensional, filling it with a heightened sense of wonder and curiosity."

By helping them to understand that each person, young or old, is a child of God and precious in his sight, this excellent book will help priests, governors, teachers and parents to understand their role in supporting our Catholic schools and their mission.

+ Malcolm McMahon OP

Right Reverend Malcolm McMahon OP
Bishop of Nottingham
Chairman of the Catholic Education Service

A HEADTEACHER'S STORY

September tops the charts for one of the worst times of the school year to discover that a member of staff is not going to turn up. To lose one is bad enough, but three in one week is a nightmare. Being an inner-city school has its challenges, but this was very unusual. Our surroundings were not the most pleasant; however, together the children and staff managed to create an environment which could only be described as an oasis of hope. Not today, though! The deputy head took over reception, I doubled up as caretaker and a governor came in to help with lunchtime supervision. Fine for a day or two, but quite another matter in the long run.

Phone calls were made to the usual supply agencies, but by 3pm there was still no caretaker. I called the agency again.

"I'm so sorry," was the answer, "but there is only one person on our books and we don't think he will be suitable."

"Why not?" I asked.

Silence.

"Well you're a Catholic school and..." Pause.

"And what difference does that make?" I asked, conscious that the tone of my voice was telling a tale.

"Well, this gentleman is not the usual sort of person you would be looking for."

"What's wrong with him?" I asked.

Pause.

"I'll send him over," she said.

An hour later the secretary came into the room and said, "The supply caretaker has arrived, but I don't think he will be staying long!"

"What do you mean? For goodness' sake show him in. He can't be that bad, can he?"

Prejudice is an awful thing and has no place in a school. But when he walked through the door I realised the agency's concern. There was not a single feature that did not have something sticking through or hanging from it. Every inch of unclad flesh seemed to be tattooed, chains hung from one side of his attire to another and a large Orthodox cross dangled around his neck. Bling, I think they call it!

"Afternoon Ma'am," he said. "You looking for a caretaker I hear."

I invited him to take a seat. He had no academic qualifications but, as he said, he had plenty of experience looking after places. His last job had been as a security man covering sick leave. At this he handed me a reference.

Never was I more pleased I had said nothing. His reference was unorthodox to say the least, stark in its brevity: "Frank is pure gold. You'll not find better."

I asked him if he had any religious background. He beamed, "Only my name. It's Francis, but Frank's more to my liking. That's why I want to come here. I know a little about being a Christian from my Nan, but I don't go to church. Tried a few times to please my Nan but got frozen out so never been back."

I showed Frank our mission statement: "We live,

love and learn together joyfully as God's family."

"What do you make of that, Frank?" I asked. His face fell.

"Well, Ma'am, looking at me, do you think the people here will accept me? I don't have much of a family, just my Nan, and I don't know anything about being a part of any other family."

Frank got the job.

Two years later the school was visited by Ofsted. Frank was singled out as one of the most outstanding contributors to the school community. Why? Because he knows what life can do to you, and especially to children in challenging circumstances. Time and time again the children told the team that Frank had "respect", and treated each one as if they were his family. Above all, he listened for as long as they wanted to talk, and was always available for everyone. Hours meant nothing. Frank was always first in and last out. "Why?" the lead inspector asked Frank. "What's hours got to do with helping your family out, mate?" was his reply.

INTRODUCTION

How to Survive Working in a Catholic School is for anyone who works in a Catholic school, or is thinking of applying for a job in one. Although Catholic schools have a great track record and are very good places to work, you may find aspects of the school and its Catholic ethos confusing. So this is designed to answer some of your questions and allay some of your concerns.

Is this book just for Catholics?

Definitely not! The 2012 census shows that 45 per cent of teachers and 50 per cent of support staff who work in Catholic schools are not Catholic.[1] But even those who have been brought up Catholic, or consider themselves practising Catholics, may have questions, or be unsure how to address the bishop when he visits. So this book is for *everyone* who works in a Catholic school. Most of us are not experts. We're just doing our best in the role we have. So it's understandable that, while you may love your job, you may have questions and concerns, or wonder if you're the only one who can see the "elephants in the room".

This book aims to be real and to deal with issues in a down-to-earth way. We'll try and keep the theology to the important points. Think of this as a practical guide to surviving (and we hope thriving!) in a Catholic school. We'll try and fill any gaps in your knowledge about the Catholic Church and its schools, so that the next time a child asks you an awkward question like: "*Sir, why don't we have meat on Fridays?*" or "*Miss, does hell really exist?*", you don't have to pretend that you're late for a staff meeting!

So is it just for teachers?

Absolutely not! Everybody who works in a Catholic school is in some way a teacher. Whether you are the headteacher, a classroom teacher, receptionist, cook, cleaner or caretaker, the children look up to you in ways you mostly won't be aware of. Children are natural copycats, they miss nothing, and are affected in some way by every encounter they have. They learn how to behave, and understand what is right and wrong, from everybody in the school. So every individual working in a Catholic school in some way represents what the school is all about.

[1] Accessed at http://cesewcensus.org.uk/downloads/Digest_of_2012_Census_Data_for_Schools_and_Colleges.pdf, 22/03/13.

This book is designed for a wide variety of readers, who between them will have a broad range of knowledge and experience of all things Catholic. So you are invited to read it however it suits you. Chapter 4, for example, deals with the subject of "Catholic Spirituality and Ethos". If you don't feel ready to tackle this, or if your immediate need is more practical (such as knowing how to address the bishop, or how to prepare for a class Mass) you will find quick-reference guides in the appendices near the back of the book, while Chapter 8 will help you to navigate your way around the church year and some of its rites and rituals. But please don't dismiss the theology, either. Although you might need to find a quiet place and devote a bit of reflection time to it, Catholic spirituality is the heart and soul of every Catholic school, and everyone who works in one – of whatever faith background or none – will find that understanding more about it will enrich them, not just in their work, but in their whole life.

Time to think and reflect

Most of us don't get much time to stop and think. The pace of life seems to be going one way: and it's fast. The technology that was supposed to make life easier seems to have made life busier. In a Catholic school it is important that everybody gets a chance to stop, catch their breath, reflect on what they're doing and try to understand in a deeper way what the mission of the school is and what part they play in it. There will be a space at the end of every chapter for reflection and prayer. We hope that this book reassures you that what you find in your Catholic school is relevant to you and your life, that you have a meaningful role to play in the school, and that at the heart of this faith is a profoundly attractive person who was and is representative of everything good. That is what we must never lose sight of when we are anxious about when to sit or stand at Mass, or how to lead a group of students in prayer.

A note about Vatican documents

From time to time we have quoted from church documents. Sometimes the titles are in Latin, but don't let that put you off. If you want to read further, you will find most of them translated into accessible English on the Vatican website: **www.vatican.va**. Chapter 6 contains a list of papal encyclicals concerning Catholic social teaching – and again most of these are available on the Vatican website.

CHAPTER 1

Help! What am I doing here?

So you work in a Catholic school: whether you've been there for ten days or ten years, there will probably have been moments when you've wondered, "*What am I doing here?*" You may be very happy in the school: it's got a great ethos, a real family atmosphere and a sense of respect among staff and students – but there may be times when you have found yourself mystified by some of the Catholic bits, and have not had the confidence to ask a question that's on your mind, or to express your opinion about something.

I'm not from a Catholic background and I'm not always sure I fit in

Don't forget that the headteacher and governors, who gave you the job, want you to be in the school, regardless of whether or not you are Catholic! Therefore you fit in because the school values your set of skills and qualities. At some level you will also have some sympathy for what the school stands for. Indeed, there aren't many people who work in Catholic schools who are anti-Catholic or anti-religious; that would be a bit strange. In fact, the word "catholic" means universal – and that's something that the Church takes very seriously. Catholics believe that we're all God's creation, whatever our background or faith, and the emphasis is on respecting difference, rather than discriminating against anyone who doesn't fit the mould. You should know and be made to feel that you are a valued member of the school community because of, not despite, your unique circumstances.

I am a baptised Catholic but that's about it. I don't always feel comfortable at work

Rest assured, you're by no means alone. For various reasons there are many people who were brought up as Catholics – baptised, educated in Catholic schools, made their first communion – and then in adulthood drifted away from the Church. The spiritual life is a journey and it is a "long and winding road". Most people who are honest about their faith will tell you that there are times of doubt and drift. It's normal. And you should not be judged by anyone on that score. Jesus was clear about that – "judge not, and you won't be judged".

But rather than living with a vague uneasiness or sense of not fitting in, why not use the opportunity to explore your faith, or revisit your Catholic heritage and give some thought to what it means to you as an adult? Be honest about those aspects of the faith that have led you to lose heart, and what is still meaningful or resonant with you. You might want a priest or catechist to work through some issues with you. You are, after all, in the best possible environment for it, so use the resources at your disposal to the full!

Once... respect and openness has been established, peoples of all religions will work together effectively for peace and mutual understanding, and so give a convincing witness before the world.

Benedict XVI[2]

I'm from another faith tradition – am I able to practise my own faith?

The Catholic Church has a "positive attitude to people and communities belonging to other religions... based on its conviction that the human race is *one*..." [1]

But much more than this, the Catholic Church emphatically believes in respecting other faiths, and calls for the inclusion of learning about and from other faiths in the religious education curriculum. *Learning about religion* and *learning from religion* are the two attainment targets for all schools – this includes other faiths.

In any school, there should be a healthy curiosity about all faiths, and you should feel able to be open about your own tradition, values, customs and practices. If you have a particular requirement that needs to be specially accommodated, that is obviously a matter of negotiation with the head-teacher and governors. What is asked of you is that you, in turn, are respectful of and engaged with the school's Catholic values.

The bar seems set very high – I'm not sure I can always live up to expectations

There's no getting away from it – the institutional Catholic Church does have some clear expectations about behaviour and choices. But at the same time, the Church is made up of individual men and women, who themselves have made choices that have often been far from perfect. It needs to be said, though, that the Church expects those who work in Catholic schools not to cause scandal or behave in a way

[1] Catholic Bishops' Conference of England and Wales, *Meeting God in Friend and Stranger*, 54 (London: Catholic Truth Society, 2010).
[2] Accessed at www.vatican.va, 08/03/13.

that undermines the values of the school. That should be written into your contract so there's no great surprise there. And it's not just the Church that would take this view. All schools these days expect an appropriate level of conduct from their staff. Again, it goes back to being role models. If you do have doubts or questions, or feel judged by anybody, you are in an excellent place to seek guidance or counselling, or just talk your feelings through. The spiritual life is a journey. None of us is perfect and never will be; we're just doing our best to grow as human beings.

Hasn't the Church had its problems in recent years?

Like each individual, the Church is also on a journey. It is a human institution and has a dark side as well as a bright side. Over the centuries there have been countless examples of inspiring Christian behaviour and plenty of examples of pretty bad behaviour, right up to the present day. But despite the wrong which has undeniably been done by some people within the Church, there are many committed Catholics who have experienced the positive side of the Church for themselves, and are determined to keep trying to make things better.

We need to keep remembering that, despite what look like a million and one rules, there is a simple message at the heart of the Catholic faith – the message of Jesus which we find in the Gospels. Catholics believe that, as the bearer of that message, the Church still has so much to offer. People are flawed and weak and make mistakes. That does not change the core message of the Gospel: to love God and love your neighbour. Some members of the Church have done great wrong, and the process of reparation and penitence – at both an individual and institutional level – will certainly take time. But if we all work towards that, the Church will become stronger, more compassionate and more relevant to the modern world.

Reflection

God has created me to do Him some definite service. He has committed some work to me which He has not committed to another. I have my mission. I may never know it in this life, but I shall be told it in the next. Somehow I am chosen for this mission, as necessary in my place as an Archangel in his – if, indeed, I fail, He can raise another, as He could make the stones children of Abraham. Yet I have a part in this great work; I am a link in a chain, a bond of connexion between persons. He has not created me for naught. I shall do good, I shall do His work; I shall be an angel of peace, a preacher of truth in my own place, while not intending it, if I do but keep His commandments and serve Him in my calling.

Blessed John Henry Newman, priest and theologian.

Wouldn't we be better off without religion and just stick to teaching?

Perhaps, if teaching was all that people needed to find happiness. The modern world tells young people that happiness can be found in getting things – wealth, celebrity, good looks. Christians believe that love, prayer and learning to follow Jesus are the routes to real, lasting peace and happiness – and many people who live committed religious lives are kept going because they have from time to time experienced moments of insight into God's love. Of course those moments are rare in the manic blur of everyday life, so when they happen they are very powerful experiences, and generations of men and women of faith have tried to describe these experiences. One of the things people describe is that everything becomes simpler and clearer, and the things that don't matter simply cease to concern us.

One of the greatest mystics, someone who was very close to God, an Englishwoman called Julian of Norwich, lived in the plague-devastated years of the fourteenth century. She is known for many wonderful sayings, including:

> *All shall be well,*
> *and all shall be well,*
> *and all manner of thing shall be well.*

This is the lovely vision that the Catholic Church believes in, and wants to try and teach our young people.

These questions and answers may or may not chime with your experience – but whatever your circumstances, beliefs or outlook, you are invited to become a full, active participant in the faith life of the school you work in – and to challenge it as an institution, and the individuals who work there, to live up to their Catholic faith. Each individual has so much potential and, whether or not you see it as God-given, it is a lifetime's work to fulfil that potential. Whatever your background or circumstances, the Catholic school should provide fertile soil for that kind of growth.

POINTS TO REMEMBER

- You are entitled to feel at home in your Catholic school – the governors appointed you, they want you there.
- You are who you are – none of us is a saint. However, we are called to be saints.
- The Church is a human organisation and people make mistakes, sometimes bad mistakes, but they are also capable of great goodness and kindness.

POINTS FOR PERSONAL REFLECTION OR GROUP DISCUSSION

- Think back to when you were appointed to the school – what led you to apply?
- Think about your own experience of faith, whether you are from a religious upbringing or not. What does faith mean to you now? What part would you like faith to play in your life in the future?
- How do you view the Church? What aspects of it do you regard as negative? Do you see these in your day-to-day experience in the school? If so, what stops you from challenging them?
- Think about some positive aspects of Church – the educational and charitable work, both at home and in the developing world (see Chapter 6). In what way do you feel you could contribute?

CHAPTER 2

What is the Catholic Church all about?

A Catholic school is supported and directed by the Catholic Church – its values and beliefs. It is, therefore, an appropriate starting point to find out about this huge and enduring institution, which claims around 1.2 billion members and is the world's largest non-government provider of education and medical services.

Whether or not you are an active member of the Catholic Church, you cannot fail to have been influenced by it. So many of the world's great thinkers and activists are or have been Catholics, and the Church's traditions, rites and language are familiar, not only within the walls of the church building, but in our wider culture and society.

A quick jaunt through history

The Church began as a small Jewish sect, distinguished from its parent group by its belief that Jesus was the Messiah, the Son of God. Following the destruction of the Temple in Jerusalem in AD 70, when Judaism had to redefine itself without sacrifice and priesthood, Jewish Christians were eventually expelled from the synagogue. They found a new home in *ekklēsia* (the church/assembly) – the community founded on Peter's recognition of Jesus as Messiah (Matthew 16:18-20).

The early Christians were clearly distinguished from their Jewish brethren in Nero's persecution following the great fire of Rome in AD 64, when two-thirds of the imperial city was destroyed. Christians were targeted as arsonists and condemned as terrorists: Christianity was made illegal throughout the Roman Empire. The struggles of the early Church were reversed when Constantine, emperor of the Western Roman Empire, and Licinius, emperor of the Eastern Roman Empire, issued the Edict of Milan in AD 313, recognising tolerance of religions throughout the whole empire. Not until AD 380, however, through Emperor Theodosius I, did Christianity become the official religion of the Roman Empire.

In 530 St Benedict wrote his rule as a practical guide for monastic community living. Great monasteries were built not only as centres of worship and learning, but also of agriculture and art and economics. Around this time there were great missionary endeavours, not least St Patrick, St Augustine of Canterbury and St Columba: the Gospel was spreading rapidly, rooting Christianity in new lands.

By the middle of the eleventh century, the East-West schism divided Christianity between the Western (Latin) branch of Christianity, which became known as the Catholic Church, and the Eastern (Greek) branch, which became known as the Orthodox

Church. Mutual excommunications were exchanged at the time, revoked only in 1965. Between the eleventh and the middle of the twelfth centuries the first universities – like Bologna and Paris and Oxford – were established and became centres of great theological learning, theology being regarded as "the queen of sciences".

The creative period of the Renaissance began in Florence, Italy, in the fourteenth century and spread throughout Europe within a hundred years. Whereas the spirit that inspired Dante (1265-1321) in his *Divine Comedy* was principally Christian, Petrarch (1304-74) was influenced largely by Humanist ideals, although he remained steadfast in his Catholic convictions. While the Renaissance began on a note of nostalgia for the classical age, it developed into a time of extraordinary innovation in painting, sculpture, architecture and writing. The Catholic Church became the greatest patron of the arts: Pope Julius II worked with Michelangelo and Raphael, commissioning such projects as the painting of the Sistine Chapel's ceiling and the frescoes of the Raphael Rooms. Julius died in 1513, four years before the beginning of the Reformation.

Paradoxically, the Reformation was triggered by a Catholic priest, an Augustinian friar named Martin Luther, in an attempt to reform the Catholic Church and free it from what he perceived as ecclesiastical malpractices – especially the sale of indulgences and the selling of clerical offices. Luther nailed his *Ninety-Five Theses on the Power and Efficacy of Indulgences* to the door of the All Saints' Church, in Wittenberg. He wanted to reform the Church from within but was excommunicated in January 1521. Other religious reformers, such as Zwingli and Calvin, followed Luther's example, but the reformers soon disagreed among themselves and divided the reform movement according to doctrinal differences, resulting in the establishment of rival Protestant churches.

The Catholic Church responded to these problems with a vigorous campaign of reform, beginning with the Council of Trent which lasted from 1545 until 1563. Among other things, the Council abolished abuses and introduced reforms affecting the sale of indulgences, the education of the clergy and the non-residence of bishops, although there was no formal concessions to Protestantism. Spiritual renewal and reform were further inspired by saints like Teresa of Avila, Francis de Sales and Philip Neri whose example and writings initiated new schools of spirituality. At the same time the new Baroque style in art, music and architecture stimulated fresh religious ardour.

From a missionary point of view, the late fifteenth and sixteenth centuries were distinguished by the dynamic spread of Catholicism to the Americas, Africa, Asia and Oceania. While the Franciscans went to Mexico, the great Spanish Jesuit, St Francis Xavier, together with Portuguese missionaries, ventured into India, Japan and Borneo.

In the seventeenth and eighteenth centuries, the Enlightenment, which elevated human reason above divine revelation, was a new challenge to the Church, as was the anti-clericalism of the French Revolution which led to the Church being outlawed and the nationalisation of its property. The end of the Napoleonic wars, in the Congress of Vienna (1814-15), brought about Catholic revival and the Papal States were restored.

(The Catholic Church and the modern world will be looked at later in this chapter.)

For all its roller-coaster history, the Church endures, and continues to have a huge impact on the lives of millions of people. And although it has experienced a bad press at times, it is, and always has been, founded on principles of compassion, love and charity – values which are deeply held by over a billion Catholics throughout the world. In Chapter 6 we will discover how these are enacted through social teaching. In the meantime, let's find out more about the Catholic Church and the schools so important to its work.

Signs and symbols

When you walk into a Catholic school you should see signs and symbols all over the place – a crucifix, depictions of Mary, a statue of the school's patron saint, religious art and stained glass etc. So why all these religious artefacts? What are they signs and symbols of? Well, before the Reformation (page 12), most churchgoers were not literate and the Church developed a very visual and tactile culture to engage and educate the faithful. An example of this can be found in St Peter's Basilica in Rome. The toe on the statue of St Peter has been worn down to a smooth stump by millions of pilgrim hands touching the saint's foot in prayer. A lot of the Protestant reformers thought this had gone too far. That is why we see to this day a number of Protestant churches stripped down, so that the focus is on the pulpit, symbolising the word of God, rather than on statues or stained glass or altar decorations. While the modern Catholic Church now appreciates the insights of other churches, it has retained its interest in art and beauty and decoration to help people appreciate the breadth of the story of faith.

What does it all mean?

From the Catholic point of view, the world is not all that it seems. There is more to reality than meets the eye. When Catholics talk about God creating the universe with a "big bang" around fourteen billion years ago (note: belief in evolution is not a problem!), this is not because they believe that God was bored and wanted to have some fun with cosmic fireworks. Catholics believe that the universe was born out of love and that God threw himself into creation in the person of Jesus. The Gospels tell us about how he lived, died and rose again in glory. Catholics believe in the presence of the risen Christ in the here and now – in the school playground, the staffroom, in each of us. And all the signs of the cross, blessings and sacraments (see Chapter 8) are signs and reminders of that.

It is heady stuff, and the truth is that Catholics have struggled since the beginning to really understand and live it. But nevertheless it is what they believe: the world, the people in it, are filled with the grace and presence of God. Theologians say that the world is *graced*. The twentieth-century American monk Thomas Merton was a great mystic. In Louisville in 1958 he had an epiphany, a kind of vision – not of heavenly beings, but rather he saw earthly beings in a heavenly light. He wrote:

There is no way of telling people that they are walking around shining like the sun... it was as if I suddenly saw the secret beauty of their hearts. If only they could all see themselves as they really are. If only we could see each other that way all the time. There would be no more war, no more cruelty, no more greed... I suppose the big problem would be that we would fall down and worship each other.[1]

What you should find in a Catholic school is a community that believes that everyone in it is filled with the love of God. It might be difficult to see it that way on a dreary Monday afternoon when Year 9 refuse to get Shakespeare, or Year 5 have had enough of your numeracy strategy, or the dining hall has been left in a complete state, again. But that is the truth of the matter. Our young people are not first and foremost "learners" or "citizens", and certainly not economic units. They have a divine origin and an eternal destiny. What you should see in school is this belief in practice – in all the policies and all the relationships. That is why Catholic schools should be places of joy and celebration. In Catholic terms, we are loved, we are saved, and life is graced and good! The challenge is to embrace this gift.

What about other schools?

What about schools that don't have a faith identity and don't talk about any of these things? Do they not regard children as special and have caring staff committed to their well-being? Are they not places of joy? Of course they are, and they are every bit as committed to the education of their students. The difference is the foundation. Some commentators argue that schools funded by the state should be neutral and not favour one religion or ethos over another, but the fact is that every school has a way of looking at the person and society which informs every policy and decision. In the Catholic school the difference is that this ideology is out in the open. In many other schools it's there, but implicit.

Some argue that Catholic schools are divisive and seek to indoctrinate young people. In those terms all schools more or less indoctrinate children, or educate them according to a world view; even if that view is "live and let live", it's a view. The Catholic school has a foundation in the Christian faith. By the nature of that foundation, the school should strive for the good, not only of its students, but for the common good of society. Many who work in Catholic schools feel a sense of personal calling to be part of such an enterprise.

[1] Thomas Merton, *Essential Writings*, Christine M. Bochen (ed.) (New York: Orbis, 2008).

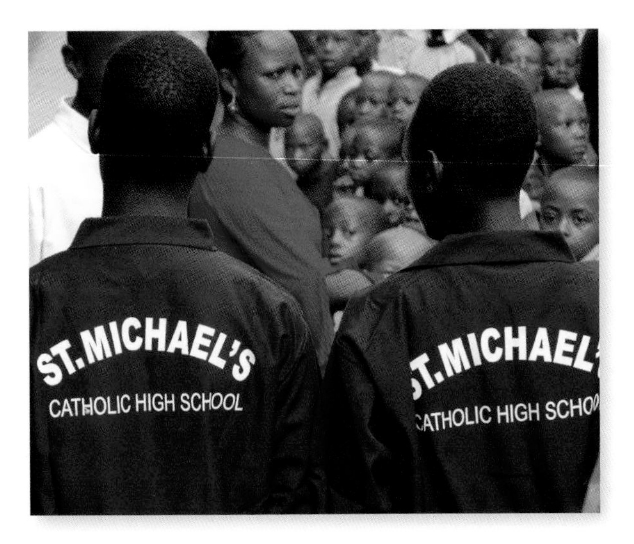

What about the rest of the world?

The Church sees its mission in the widest sense of the "common good". There is a strong commitment to the world's poor, reinforced by the pronouncements of Pope Francis, which is spelled out in a number of documents, and the stated desire is that "the goods of creation... may be more equitably distributed among all men and women" (Dogmatic Constitution on the Church, 36). There's not much room for ambiguity there. This is known as Catholic social teaching. In many ways it's our best-kept secret (more of that in Chapter 6). But the message goes right back to the Gospel and the passion Jesus showed for the poor and marginalised. This is why in all Catholic schools you should find a serious commitment to charitable activity, and why many Catholic organisations are devoted to alleviating poverty. This teaching reminds us that even though Catholics believe in a "graced nature" (or as the Jesuit priest-poet Gerard Manley Hopkins put it, "the world is charged with the grandeur of God"), they know that everything is far from perfect and are challenged to do what they can to be agents of change.

The Catholic Church meets the modern world – Vatican II

We mentioned earlier that the Church doesn't always live up to its ideals because it is full of human beings. However, the Church believes that it is guided on its journey by the Holy Spirit (see the section on the Holy Trinity in Chapter 4), and from time to time the windows are thrown open and the fresh air of God comes rushing in, as it did in the early 1960s, when Pope John XXIII called a Council of the Church. This is known as the Second Vatican Council, or Vatican II. All the world's bishops gathered in Rome for four enormous meetings between 1962 and 1965. We can't go into everything that was said, but it did bring about remarkable change, and to this day the Church is seeking to understand and implement those changes.

Before the Second Vatican Council, most altars in the churches were oriented to the east, the place of the rising sun, in celebration of Jesus' resurrection in Jerusalem. Thus when Mass was celebrated both priest and people faced the same direction – eastwards. Also most Catholics were taught that there was no salvation outside the Church; lay people (non-clergy) did not have much of an active role in the liturgy. The Church saw itself as something of a fortress of truth in a hostile and sinful world. So much of that thinking changed with Vatican II. The Church turned towards the world in a spirit of friendship and solidarity. The Council fathers recognised that grace is present in the hearts of all people and that anyone trying to live a good life is moved by that. With the new liturgical changes, Mass was celebrated more and more *versus populum* (facing the people) and in the language of the people, and there was a growing recognition of the importance of the role of lay people in the life of the Church.

The Church thinks in centuries

You may well ask why the Church doesn't quite feel like that at the moment. Well, one response to that is, "the Church thinks in centuries... not in decades". This line comes from the 1963 movie *The Cardinal*. We are used to living in a culture of instant responses and short-term action plans – we get twitchy if we haven't had an instant reply to our email, and our schools have not escaped that culture. The pace in most schools is frenetic, we are governed by action plans and performance measures, which makes it all the harder to hang onto that vision – and all the more important that we do.

The Church scans a horizon from the beginning of time to the end, so the time which has passed since the beginning of the Vatican Council is like the blink of an eye. Liberals within the Church are frustrated that the pace of change has not been quicker, while traditionalists think that Vatican II went too far and want to slow things down. Like any community or organisation founded on belief, there is a great spectrum of temperament and opinion.

So what about Jesus?

There is an ancient Chinese saying that when a finger points at the moon, only a fool looks at the finger. The Church is the finger pointing at God-in-Jesus, and that is its reason for being. On the last day of his life, Pope John Paul I is reported as saying, "It is Jesus alone we must present to the world. Outside of this, we have no reason to exist." And it is Jesus we must never lose sight of in our schools. At the heart of all the theology and interesting facts and facets of the Church, Jesus Christ is the reason for the Christian faith, and a commitment to his kingdom is what Christians work towards – and this kingdom is radically different from the way the world thinks.

Jesus in the Gospels is a powerful and compelling character. Young people in schools respond warmly to this extraordinary figure, who had such a passion for the poor and marginalised, who wasn't afraid to take on the religious leaders of the day, whose response to the sinner was always to forgive, even if they didn't ask for forgiveness. He did not lord it over people, he did not set out to create a grand institution, he did not write anything down or draw up a list of rules to follow. He told stories about the kingdom and reign of God. He healed people. He made friends. He turned the thinking of the world on its head and the truth is that Christians have struggled ever since to come to terms with what Jesus represents.

Where am I in all this?

Do you have to believe all of the above in order to work in a Catholic school? And what about the Catechism (a summary of the doctrine of the Catholic Church)? The answer is that you certainly don't have to be a fully paid-up subscriber. In fact, there will be many people working in Catholic schools who don't know much about the Catechism, and as we said earlier you're not expected to be an expert. You may be sitting there at a school Mass or an assembly thinking, *"I'm really not sure I get this, or even believe it"* – and you would not be alone. We are all on a journey and we are all at very different stages of that journey.

Those who work in a Catholic school should certainly respect and support what the Catholic school is all about, and those who are in what are known as "reserved posts" (the headteacher, deputy head, head of religious education and RE co-ordinator) must have more knowledge and be committed to the practice of the faith. But for most staff who work in Catholic schools there is no requirement to tick every box. You should of course be committed to developing and to being personally and professionally as good as you can be in your role in the school. But above all there is an expectation that you are willing to be with the young people on their journey.

POINTS TO REMEMBER

- There are shades of opinion in the Catholic Church, just as everywhere. But beneath it there's a core message – and it's all about Jesus.
- The Church thinks in centuries; it's not a modern media-savvy corporation. It thinks in "big picture" terms.
- You're on a journey – and right now you're here because you've been chosen.

POINTS FOR PERSONAL REFLECTION OR GROUP DISCUSSION

- Can you understand why around 1.2 billion people are practising Catholics?
- What did you know about the Catholic Church before you took the job, and what was your main source of knowledge?
- Did you have any experience – positive or negative – of the Catholic Church? If you have questions about it, where might you go for answers?
- Are you aware of Catholic social teaching, which is at the heart of Catholic teaching? If not you might want to turn to Chapter 6 to find out more.

Reflection

THE DREAM OF GOD

The Lord God said: I myself will dream
a dream within you;
Good dreaming comes from me, you know.
My dreams seem impossible,
Not too practical
Nor for the cautious man or woman;
A little risky sometimes,
A trifle brash perhaps...
Some of my friends prefer
To rest more comfortably in sounder sleep
with visionless eyes...
But from those who share my dreams
I ask a little patience, a little humour,
Some small courage, and a listening heart –
I will do the rest...
Then they will risk and wonder at their
daring;
Run – and marvel at their speed...
Build – and stand in awe at the beauty of
their building.
You will meet me often as you work in your
companions who share the risk,
In your friends who believe in you enough
To lend their own dreams,
Their own hands,
Their own hearts, to your building.
In the people who will stand in your doorway,
Stay awhile, and walk away knowing that
they too
Can find a dream...
There will be sun-filled days
And sometimes a little rain.
A little variety! Both come from me.
So come now – be content.
It is my dream you dream,
My house you build,
My caring you witness;
My love you share
And this is the heart of the matter.

Charles Péguy

CHAPTER 3

What is a Catholic school and how is it different?

Working in a Catholic school is very different from working in one that is not Catholic – indeed, we hope it is! But of course all schools have a great deal in common when it comes to day-to-day aspects of running and working in them. Like any school, a Catholic school has its challenges – the demands of the teaching curriculum jostle alongside the need to keep to timetables, provide nutritious food at mealtimes, occasionally juggle classrooms, stick to budgets, take health and safety into account, and provide sport and extracurricular activities. So many young people growing up together makes a Catholic school, like any other, a challenging and hopefully rewarding place to work.

Of course, you know all this already. But the point is that just because a Catholic school is built upon a strong Christian foundation, it doesn't make the day-to-day logistics any easier to manage. Also, it doesn't make it a rarefied place, and it doesn't necessarily make the people that work in it any holier than anyone else.

So what is different about a Catholic school?

A Catholic school should have a clear purpose and be informed by beliefs and values that are rooted in scripture and church teachings. These should permeate every aspect of day-to-day learning and life in the school. They should not be based on coercion, or on rules for their own sake, but should spring from the school's ethos of justice, forgiveness, love and compassion as found in the Gospel (for more on this see Chapters 4 and 6).

If we want to identify the distinguishing features that make a Catholic school different, we need to ask the question, why does it exist? Well, for one thing, a Catholic school is part of the mission of the worldwide Catholic Church. As such, it exists:

- to witness to the mission, beliefs and values of Jesus Christ.
- because each child is a God-given gift that the world is waiting for and needs.
- to teach young people to acquire critical thinking skills, write and speak articulately and discover their God-given talents and vocation.
- to inspire them to recognise who their God is, who they are, and discover the reason for their existence on earth.
- to motivate young people to become people of challenge, change and transformation:

  Challenge: to see the world as God created it to be and not as the prevailing culture of the time dictates; to be unafraid and unashamed to challenge anything which denigrates or belittles the person; to see every person as a brother or sister made in the image and likeness of God. And, with this at the heart of their learning, not to tolerate anything less.

Change: to be agents of and advocates for change where it is needed; to understand how to bring about change wisely, bravely and peacefully; not to be afraid to persevere when the going gets tough.

Transformation: to be personally transformed and, through that transformation, able to see the world from God's perspective and work towards a vision of a transformed world; to be ablaze with the fire of the Holy Spirit (see Chapter 4), burning to create a world of justice and peace for all.

Not just a place for learning

As you can see, the Gospel message and the example of Jesus underpin each of these points – and *that* is the key difference between a Catholic school and any other. You will think that they are very high ideals – and indeed they are – but that is what our schools are founded for.

In line with these ideals and this uncompromising spirit, a Catholic school should be a "big picture" place – a living community where everyone is educated in heart and soul, as well as mind. Following Jesus' example, it should be a place where everyone is equally respected and unconditionally loved, a community which wants to reach out to all, especially the poor and marginalised, and those in greatest need (for more on this see Chapter 6 on Catholic social teaching). While we recognise that there are many very good schools, staffed by very good people (many of whom, of course, will be informed in their work by their faith), we also believe that education is infinitely richer for having these Christian ideals at its heart.

To put it simply: a Catholic school is where life, faith and culture are one.

Questions are probably rising in your mind as you read: Is this really possible? Could a school in this country be that good, that revolutionary? What about Ofsted?

So are Catholic schools any good?

Yes, they are very good, and improving, as they strive for excellence in all categories. Research into school performance shows that Catholic schools and colleges are continuing to outperform national averages. The following figures are taken from the Catholic Education Service's Digest of 2014 Census Data for Schools and Colleges, which in turn quotes from a variety of sources, including the Ofsted 2013-14 Annual Report:

- 83 per cent of Catholic primary schools have Ofsted grades of good or outstanding (81 per cent nationally).
- At the age of 11, pupils in Catholic schools outperform national average English and maths SATs scores by 5 per cent.
- At GCSE level, Catholic schools outperform the national average by 8 per cent.

With 2,156 Catholic schools and colleges educating 816,007 pupils, and employing 47,986 teachers and approximately 39,102 support staff, that is an awful lot of schools, pupils and staff living and learning together, to a level which is already above national averages.

You might think that these results are connected to privilege: *"Aren't most Catholic schools primarily attended by white middle-class kids?"* So you may be surprised to learn that 19.2 per cent of pupils at Catholic primary schools in England and Wales live in the most deprived areas (compared with 12 per cent from maintained schools). The secondary school data is broadly the same. In addition, Catholic schools are more ethnically diverse than national averages (36 per cent of Catholic primary school pupils are from ethnic minority backgrounds, compared with 30 per cent nationally).

Catholic schools in Scotland and Northern Ireland are also well known for their high academic standards and holistic approach to learning. In 1998 First Minister Alex Salmond summed up the value of having Catholic schools in the Scottish education system:

I am proud to support Catholic education in Scotland... The point is not merely that Catholic schools get good results. They do, of course, and that is vital. What also matters is that children in Catholic schools gain a wider sense of responsibility and identity – and a desire to help improve the community in which they live.[2]

What does the Church say about Catholic schools?

One of the key documents produced by the Second Vatican Council (see Chapter 2) was the Declaration on Christian Education. Issued by Pope Paul VI on 28 October 1965, it makes it clear that the Church takes education extremely seriously, and regards Catholic schools as agents for social cohesion and change – not just among Catholics, but for the good of *all* people. Don't be put off by the sometimes stilted language, and do bear in mind how radical this was for the Church in 1965:

All people of whatever race, condition or age,
in virtue of their dignity as human persons,
have an inalienable right to education.

Declaration on Christian Education, 1

Therefore, a Catholic school has a responsibility to promote and further education. Again, note how inclusive this is in spirit:

The school is of outstanding importance. In nurturing the intellectual faculties which is its special mission, it develops a capacity for sound judgement and introduces the pupils to the cultural heritage bequeathed to them by former generations. It fosters a sense of values and prepares them for professional life. By providing for friendly contacts between pupils of different characters and backgrounds it encourages mutual understanding.

Declaration on Christian Education, 5

Not only that, but all Catholics are to take this responsibility extremely seriously and support schools however they can:

The sacred synod earnestly exhorts the pastors of the church and all the faithful to spare no sacrifice in helping Catholic schools to become increasingly effective.

Declaration on Christian Education, 9

[2] Cardinal Winning Education Lecture, marking the start of Catholic Education Week.

A more recent church document was published in 1997, showing how highly the Church continues to regard education in the broadest sense of the word:

The Catholic school should be able to offer young people the means to acquire the knowledge they need in order to find a place in a society which is strongly characterised by technical and scientific skill. But at the same time, it should be able, above all, to impart a solid Christian formation.

The Catholic School on the Threshold of the Third Millennium, 8

The document goes on to quote Pope John Paul II, emphasising that this spirit of inclusivity is not simply the Church's ethos, but part of Christ's teaching:

The Catholic school sets out to be a school for the human person and of human persons. "The person of each individual human being, in his or her material and spiritual needs, is at the heart of Christ's teaching: this is why the promotion of the human person is the goal of the Catholic school."

The Catholic School on the Threshold of the Third Millennium, 9

You can begin to see how it all fits together. We are here to do the very best we can for the pupils in our care in every aspect of life and, as an integral part of this, we have a responsibility to ensure that they in turn become people who want to build a better world for all people.

A (very) brief history of Catholic schools in Britain

Catholic schools have been in existence in Britain since the sixth century, when they were founded by cathedrals and monasteries to educate priests and monks and train choristers in music. Religious orders and congregations also provided for poor children, while wealthy philanthropists were keen to support education, and often founded schools.

For over three hundred years after the Reformation in the sixteenth century (see Chapter 2) being a Catholic in Britain was a perilous business. Things changed with the 1829 Catholic Emancipation Act, which paved the way for Catholics once again to educate their children and, in particular, poor people. 1847 saw the establishment of the Catholic Poor School Committee, which distributed the first government grants towards building Catholic schools and training colleges for teachers. In 1850 Pope Pius IX re-established twenty-two dioceses in England and Wales and in 1852 the bishops met at the Synod of Westminster, to restore the church hierarchy. Education was top of the agenda, and building schools was prioritised over places of worship:

Wherever there may seem to be an opening for a new mission, we would prefer the erection of a school, so arranged as to serve temporarily for a chapel, to that of a church without one.[3]

In 1905 the Catholic Education Council (nowadays known as the Catholic Education Service) was established to promote Catholic education in England and Wales. By the end of the nineteenth century education had been made compulsory for children

[3] Westminster Provincial Synod, 17 July 1852. Accessed at **www.st-edmunds.richmond.sch.uk/Governing%20a%20Catholic%20School.pdf**, 11/02/13.

up to twelve years of age, although many families struggled to pay the fees. At the same time, grants were provided for church schools (both Catholic and Church of England). This really angered some, who felt that taxpayers' money should not be used for the education of a few.

The debate raged until the 1944 Education Act (also known as the Butler Act) finally gave all children in England and Wales the right to free education funded by local rates and government grants. The Act created Voluntary Aided Schools, meaning that faith-based schools became part of the state system of education, while being able to retain their distinctive ethos. Church schools had to contribute financially, and were usually part-funded by the diocese or a religious order. But gradually the government has picked up more and more of the costs of Voluntary Aided Schools, to the present amount of 90 per cent.[4]

In Scotland, school fees had been largely abolished in 1890, although those attending Catholic schools had to pay for their education up until 1918, when they too became state funded.

That faith-based schools are deemed worthy of public funds is a great acknowledgement of the value of education built on religious foundations. So we must continue to earn that recognition and privileged status, by being good stewards of public funds.

Who goes to a Catholic school?

Entry into a Catholic school is according to the individual school's admissions criteria. Catholic schools were established to educate baptised Roman Catholics, and the majority of pupils fall into this category. But having said that, many schools are very happy to admit pupils from other Christian denominations and faith backgrounds – or no faith background at all. Catholic schools recognise that we are all part of God's family, though following

different paths, and everyone working or studying in a Catholic school should feel that they are part of a welcoming and inclusive family, where diversity is recognised and celebrated.

[4] The government contributes 100% of the revenue funding to Voluntary Aided Catholic Schools, while the Church – which usually owns the buildings – contributes 10% of its overall budget for the purposes of capital funding, generally building works and maintenance. This does not apply to academies.

What really matters is that those who go to a Catholic school and their parents or carers know and understand the school's purpose and mission, and are comfortable with the idea of learning and living in this environment.

Different models of Catholic school

The Church recognises that a Catholic school may assume various models or roles according to local circumstances:

The Catholic school is to take on different forms in keeping with local circumstances. Thus the Church considers very dear to her heart those Catholic schools, found especially in the areas of the new churches, which are attended also by students who are not Catholics.

Declaration on Christian Education, 9

Model 1: The majority of pupils and staff are practising Catholics. Home, school and parish work closely together.
Model 2: The headteacher and senior leaders are Catholic, but many of the pupils and staff may not be. Here the Church is responding to the rise of secularisation of society and materialism.
Model 3: The headteacher and senior leaders are practising Catholics, but there may be very few Christians living in the local area. Here the school acts as a means of witnessing to Jesus and the Gospel.

Which is the best model?
It is not a matter of best, but responding to the need. The Church exists for mission – and to evangelise – in other words, to tell, show, witness and reveal to all people who God is, who they are, and how much they are loved. This is called proclaiming the good news.

What is the good news?
The good news is that God so loved the world – and you – that in spite of the fact that his children were making such a mess of everything he would not abandon them. When life on earth is at an all-time low, God sends his Son, Jesus, as a human being. He is born, lives, dies and rises again to show us once and for all just who we are, how much we are loved and how to live and love as he did.

So wherever there is a need, the Church will go first to those in the greatest need, and support a Catholic school there, in order to witness to this message. It is not a matter of opening a Catholic school and forcing people to be Catholics. The role of the Catholic school is to educate, because education sets you free. What each person does with the knowledge and experiences they receive through working or studying at a Catholic school is up to them.

How is working in a Catholic school different?

As we saw at the beginning of this chapter, many of the day-to-day aspects of your work will not be substantially different from working in any other school. In other chapters we will look at the National Curriculum, and see how the school's daily life and the teaching and learning throughout the community may be affected by the school's Catholic foundation.

The word education has two Latin root words. One is "educere", meaning "to lead forth", or "to lead out of". The other root word is "educare", meaning "to support and nurture".

The future of humanity lies in the hands of those who are strong enough to provide coming generations with reasons for living and hoping.

Pastoral Constitution on the Church in the Modern World, 31

A key difference when you work in a Catholic school is that you – whatever your own faith, background or views – are invited and encouraged to contribute to the school's whole ethos. If you are not a Catholic or a Christian, this may come as a surprise. But don't be tempted to compartmentalise your contribution or get into the mindset of "*I'm just here to teach – I leave the religious bit to other people.*" Remember that everyone in any school is in some way a teacher. In the light of the Catholic Church's views on the vital importance of education (see page 23), and by virtue of the fact that the headteacher and school governors have given you the job, you are deemed to be someone who can enrich the faith life of the school and community.

So what does that mean? Well, it has nothing to do with converting to Catholicism or forcing you to believe anything. It has everything to do with being fully engaged with your work and your work environment, and knowing that you have a significant contribution to make in every aspect of the school's life – including its faith life.

Is there anyone who should not work in a Catholic school?

Yes – the cynic with a closed mind, who refuses to engage with questions of faith. It would be unwise for anyone to apply to a Catholic school if they felt unable to support what the school is all about, because they would feel unhappy and ill at ease in their work. In turn, the pupils would pick this up and it would undermine the school's aims and mission.

If you accept a post in a Catholic school you should be comfortable with the whole package – the way of life, thinking and being. That's not to say that you're not allowed to question or challenge anything (pupils are not the only ones learning in school!), but it is important to spend time reflecting on the important questions of spirituality and ethos, and the part they play in your life. In the next chapter we will explore Catholic spirituality and ethos in more depth.

Prayer

In all our travelling

All: May your footsteps guide us

In our journeying to work and returning

All: May your footsteps guide us

Within our homes and families

All: May your footsteps guide us

In our leisure time together

All: May your footsteps guide us

In difficult situations and conflict

All: May your footsteps guide us

As we stumble on the way

All: May your footsteps guide us

In the travelling of our faith

All: May your footsteps guide us

As we place our trust in you

All: May your footsteps guide us

In all our travelling, Lord,
may it be your footsteps
in which we place our feet.

POINTS TO REMEMBER

- Don't worry if you don't understand everything that is going on in your school – that's normal. Just ask someone who knows!
- You are part of something bigger than your school.
- What you are doing is valued and supported from the very top of the Church.
- It is OK to be where you are today in your life journey. Tomorrow you will be in a different place, and that is OK too.
- The foundation stone of a Catholic school is not a book, a set of rules or guidelines, although they all exist – it is first and foremost a person, Jesus Christ.

POINTS FOR PERSONAL REFLECTION OR GROUP DISCUSSION

- What has surprised you in this chapter?
- In what ways has it helped you to understand why you are here?
- Do you think you could explain to someone else why the Catholic Church is so committed to education?
- Of the three models of Catholic school outlined on page 26, which one best fits your school? How do you feel about that?
- To what extent do you think your school is achieving the mission of the Catholic Church and how?

CATCH IT
BIN IT
Tricks Stork
Dan did not.
Dan got in.

CHAPTER 4

Catholic spirituality and ethos

In the last chapter we looked at what makes a Catholic school different. In this chapter we will take a closer look at one vitally important aspect of that difference.

Most people in our secular day and age go about their daily business without giving much thought to the "big questions" in life. Christians, however, believe we are infinitely richer if we do face those questions, and in doing so acknowledge that we are spiritual beings.

You may protest: *"But I took this job because I need to support my family and it's near to where I live – what's that got to do with being spiritual?"*

Spirituality isn't confined to the clergy or pious people – or Christians or even Catholics. Whether we know it or not, we are all spiritual beings, longing for fulfilment and purpose in our lives. We are all graced, remember... The difference, however, is that Christians believe that spirituality, based on the person of Jesus and his teachings, is the driving force, the expression of all that we are and do, think and feel.

Engaging with the big questions sometimes means facing difficult realities that we would prefer to ignore – forgiveness, for example, or death. Just pause for a moment to think about how those two things have affected you. It's little wonder that people choose to live on the surface of life and opt for all kinds of distractions. By contrast, Christians believe that if we embrace spirituality, every aspect of life acquires new meaning and real purpose. Life might not be easier – but it will be richer, deeper, more fulfilling and worthwhile.

You may ask: *"But I'm just a cook / a teaching assistant / a caretaker / a physics teacher – what's that got to do with being spiritual?"*

In a Catholic school there is no such thing as a secular education. Learning is a sacred endeavour, and all learning helps us to fathom the mysteries of life. (Notice the use of that word "fathom" – not "answer" or "solve". There are many mysteries we will never get to the bottom of, and nobody pretends to have all the answers.)

When we say "learning is a sacred endeavour", that doesn't mean that spirituality is confined to the classroom or formal education. That is because Christians see every activity, every moment, as an opportunity to learn – that includes meals, break times, the journey to school, the journey home, and every waking and sleeping moment in between.

Whether you are a cook, teaching assistant, caretaker or teacher, the idea of integrating spirituality into your work might seem daunting,

Often we want to be
somewhere other
than where we are,
or even to be someone
other than who we are...
It is very important
to realise that
our vocation is hidden
in where we are
and who we are...
We are good enough to do
what we are called to do.
Be yourself!

Henri J.M. Nouwen[1]

but it means that your job ceases to be "just a job", and becomes a vocation, and you start to see that you are engaged in something much bigger. And it doesn't have to involve a huge personal change. We complicate our lives so much that becoming switched on to our spiritual side is actually, by contrast, blissfully simple. It's not about adding or achieving anything, but letting go and relaxing into being who we really are.

Brothers and sisters in Christ

In much the same way that Christians see every moment as precious and interconnected, so they believe that each individual is priceless (see Luke 12:6-7), and that all people are deeply connected. We are all part of God's family as brothers and sisters, and what happens to you happens to me. So you will hear expressions such as:

- Everyone belongs to the people of God.
- Together we make up the Body of Christ.
- We are all called to live in communion.

Often when we hear expressions like this we dismiss them as impossible – things that would be good in a perfect world. Sure, all Catholics don't go around feeling totally "at one" with each other – at times you'll see disharmony and discord in your school, just as you would in any other. But there is an underlying ideal and a heartfelt belief that we are all connected even if we don't act as though we are, and that with practice and faith we can experience this for ourselves.

If we start to recognise the connection between ourselves and other people we start to see others as God sees them – beautiful, amazing, full of grace

[1] Henri J.M. Nouwen, *Bread for the Journey: Reflections for Every Day of the Year* (London: Darton, Longman & Todd, 1996).

and possibilities. In the context of a Catholic education, then, the challenge is to help children and young people discover their full potential. Of course, nobody appears beautiful or particularly good all the time – this is the ongoing challenge! But you are working in an environment where striving to meet this challenge is not just desirable – it is essential. It is a core reason for the very existence of the school and everyone within it.

Blessed Pope John Paul II called for all educators to make this sense of connectedness their guiding principle – calling it "a spirituality of communion" (At the Beginning of the New Millennium, 43). This is an awesome vision which should permeate the life of the Catholic school. In practice it means an end to everything that belittles or diminishes the humanity of another person.

There is no longer Jew or Greek,
there is no longer slave or free,
there is no longer male and female;
for all of you are one in Christ Jesus.

Galatians 3:28

Catholic schools have a long tradition of pastoral care

Pastoral care is central to the ethos and identity of a Catholic school. The patron saint of teachers, St Jean-Baptiste de La Salle, who lived and worked in education over three hundred years ago, stressed the need for teachers to "touch hearts". This was so that each pupil felt that they mattered and were valued as unique and loved. This individual and important approach was to demonstrate that those who cared for young people did so with the development of the whole person as a high priority. Of course, any good school will have a caring and professional pastoral care system. The difference in a Catholic school is that the foundation and inspiration for the care offered to the students come from a commitment to the Gospel and the person of Jesus Christ. It may not feel like it on a wet Monday afternoon in January, but what is being offered to that Year 5 boy in distress, or that Year 9 girl in confusion, is no less than the love of God in human form. The pastoral system in the Catholic school is not there just to pick up the pieces when things go wrong, but to actively promote the flourishing of the students.

What is Christian spirituality?

Theologians discuss and debate what spirituality is – but a useful working definition is that spirituality is seeking to know God, rather than seeking to know about God. But it's also practical – in other words, our spirituality can be defined as the reason why we do what we do and the way in which we do it. We act in a particular way because of what we believe about the purpose and meaning of life. The greatest and most powerful aspect of a person is their spirit.

Some teachings of Jesus that appear in the Gospels of Matthew and Luke, known as the Beatitudes, are a good starting point for thinking about spirituality. The word "beatitude" comes from the Latin *beatus,* which means "happy", "fortunate", or "blissful". In the Beatitudes, Jesus gives us a vision of what we might call "spirituality in action":

Blessed are the poor in spirit, for theirs is the kingdom of heaven.
Blessed are those who mourn, for they will be comforted.
Blessed are the meek, for they will inherit the earth.
Blessed are those who hunger and thirst for righteousness, for they will be filled.
Blessed are the merciful, for they will receive mercy.
Blessed are the pure in heart, for they will see God.
Blessed are the peacemakers, for they will be called children of God.
Blessed are those who are persecuted for righteousness' sake, for theirs is the kingdom of heaven.

Matthew 5:3-10

In an age when people equated wealth, power and being busy with virtue, this was radical, subversive spirituality, and a rousing call to live peacefully and humbly with one another – a vision of a life filled with compassion and love. Two thousand years later, Jesus' teachings have been so influential that they underpin our ideas about social justice and morality – not just for Catholics, but in the wider cultural context. Most of us, whatever our faith or background, are profoundly influenced by this amazing man, who stood on a mountain all those years ago and turned conventional thinking on its head.

The Holy Trinity

Catholic spirituality is rooted in the Holy Trinity – the source and centre of Christian faith, and generally acknowledged to be a very difficult teaching to comprehend! Indeed it is, and always will be, pure mystery. But at the same time it is absolutely fundamental to the faith. Many people who have spent time reflecting on it find it breathtaking, a mystery full of beauty. The word "trinity" has its origins in the Latin for "three", and the study of the Holy Trinity is about the relationship between three "persons" (as they are known by the Church) – God the Father, God the Son, and God the Holy Spirit. One way to think about this is through an image:

Andrei Rublev was a medieval Russian artist, famous for painting icons (see the glossary) and frescoes. He, like many artists through the ages, was captivated by this idea of the "one in three" mystery of the Trinity, and this image was his way of expressing it. It actually depicts an Old Testament story, in which three angels visited Abraham (see Genesis 18:1-15), but at the same time it is generally considered to be a depiction of the Holy Trinity. It is thought that the figure on the left depicts God the Father, while the middle figure is Jesus the Son of God (the colours of the tunic symbolise Christ's human blood and royal status), while the figure on the right in green is the Holy Spirit. On the table lies a dish containing the meat that Abraham and Sarah prepared for their guests. The dish stands at the very centre of the circular arrangement, and is thought to symbolise the Eucharist (see Chapter 8).

The big question about the Trinity concerns the relationship between these three persons, and their relationship in turn with humanity. Note that in the Rublev depiction each of them has an identical face, to indicate that they are of equal status. Notice too that they are neither male nor female in appearance. Each looks lovingly towards the other, with an empty place at the table for "me".

Another helpful way to understand the Trinity comes from the Early Years Foundation Stage, where this very difficult concept is brilliantly explained by teachers. They make the sign of the cross and, as they touch their forehead, they say:

Dear God may all my thinking and learning
(hand on forehead to symbolise God the Father)
all my loving
(hand on heart – Jesus the Son)
and everything I do today
(touching either shoulder – the Holy Spirit)
be my best for you.

In the Gospels Jesus speaks about himself, the Father and the Holy Spirit and their unique relationship with each other – although he never specifically mentions the "Trinity". In the Gospel of John (for example, 10:30 and 14:26), it becomes clear that these relationships are very different from human relationships. These persons of the Trinity are not human but divine, and make up the "substance" of God.

You may ask, *"So what do you mean by God having 'substance'?"*

Many people think of God as ethereal – heavenly and other-worldly. But when God sent his beloved son Jesus on earth to live among us, when God's Word became flesh or incarnate, it called for a radical new way of thinking and talking about God. In the three hundred years following Jesus' life on earth, theologians and scholars deliberated about who exactly he had been. Had he been a prophet, a mortal man with exceptional powers, a god, or something else? Was he made of flesh and blood like you and me, or physically different? And importantly, what was the precise nature of his relationship with God? This branch of theology is known as Christology, and the theology of the Trinity is intertwined with questions about Jesus Christ.

In your work you will come across the Trinity in the school in a variety of ways – not least the churches and schools named after it – while of course Trinity Sunday is a particular celebration of the Holy Trinity. In addition, when people recite the Creed (a summary of core beliefs), much of what they say is describing the nature of the Trinity. You will often hear the "Trinitarian formula" used in worship and the liturgy (public worship). This comes from the Gospel of Matthew (28:19), when Jesus instructed his disciples to go and make disciples of all nations, baptising them "in the name of the Father, and of the Son, and of the Holy Spirit". So even if you are baffled by the mystery of the Holy Trinity, when you hear these beautiful words, you might want to pause to reflect on the awesome mystery that lies behind it!

What is Catholic ethos?

You may well hear talk of the school's "Catholic ethos", and you may wonder what that is – and you won't be the first to have done so. Monsignor Marcus Stock offers a helpful definition:

*The word "ethos" comes from a Greek word (**εθοσ**) meaning "custom" or "habit"... an "ethos" is a way of living, behaving and doing things by people who, though diverse, follow common values and are united by a shared vision of life. It is often therefore used in a way that is closely linked with "culture" and "philosophy".*[2]

Much as we can think of the Beatitudes (see page 33) as "spirituality in action", we experience ethos in the way in which someone expresses themselves through their practices, way of life, and how they relate to other people.

In 1999 the government came up with the idea that every school in England and Wales should have an ethos statement to give it energy and focus. Of course, this was not a new concept for Christian schools, but it was an additional level of bureaucracy. So the Catholic Education Service offered governors of Catholic schools a recommendation to help them fulfil their obligation. The suggested statement shows what an enormous challenge it is to run a Catholic school, and gives an insight into the competing and sometimes conflicting pressures that the headteacher and governors are under:

The school was founded by and is part of the Catholic Church. The school is to be conducted as a Catholic school in accordance with Canon Law and teachings of the Roman Catholic Church... in particular:

- religious education is to be in accordance with the teachings, doctrines, discipline and general and particular norms of the Catholic Church;
- religious worship is to be in accordance with the rites, practices, discipline and liturgical norms of the Catholic Church;
- at all times the school is to serve as a witness to the Catholic faith in Our Lord Jesus Christ.[3]

The school mission statement

An individual school's ethos is defined in its mission statement. Any organisation needs some kind of mission statement to give it cohesion and purpose.

[2] Marcus Stock, *Christ at the Centre: Why the Church Provides Catholic Schools*, p. 18. (London: Catholic Truth Society, 2013).
[3] Ethos Statement for Catholic Schools in England and Wales, 1999 to present. Accessed at **http://www.portsmouthdiocese.org.uk/schools/governors_of_catholic_schools.php**, 22/03/13.

A mission statement should take into account the questions: "Who are we?", "Why are we here?", and "What are we here to be and do?" Here are some examples of Catholic schools' mission statements:

Following Jesus' footsteps and inspired by St Robert Southwell we work hard, aim high and treat everyone with honesty and gentleness.

St Robert Southwell Primary School, London

In our Catholic community we aim to work with our young people to help each of them fulfil their individual potential and enrich their lives.

All Saints Secondary School, Glasgow

We, through our catholic ethos, promise Christian values, academic and vocational excellence, and the personal development of every pupil in a caring, happy and welcoming environment.

Lismore Comprehensive School, Northern Ireland

Note how far-reaching these statements are in intention, and how inclusive and loving their language is. It is clear that each of these schools is about far more than simply getting good academic results. Of course those matter, but if a school reduces its mission to results at all costs, then it should sound alarm bells and raise questions: *"What is being neglected?"*, *"Is the mission of the Church being carried out?"*, *"Has another agenda crept in?"*

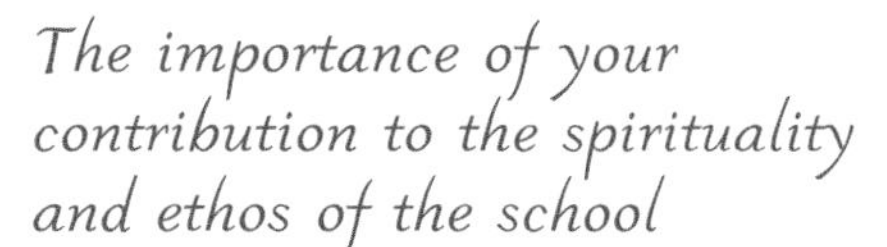

The importance of your contribution to the spirituality and ethos of the school

A Catholic school is not just a collection of individuals, or a factory for churning out students with good academic grades, but a community that witnesses to a common vision and mission. The young people who come to the school to learn, come not as empty vessels to be filled with knowledge but, through their relationship with you and each other, to discover what it is to be human and the place God has in their lives.It should be clear to you by now that this doesn't mean you have to personally assent to every statement of belief, but you must recognise and appreciate the ethos of the school and value the school as a place which is underpinned by and imbued with a sense of Christian spirituality.

POINTS TO REMEMBER

- Keep it simple. You are already a fully spiritual being. What is important is that you accept the ethos of the school.
- You are on a journey and it will last a lifetime!
- Identify someone in your school that you feel you can go to clarify anything you don't understand.
- Begin where you are and never mind where anyone else seems to be.

POINTS FOR PERSONAL REFLECTION OR GROUP DISCUSSION

- Has this chapter enabled you to reflect on your own spirituality? Have you seen anything in a new or different way?
- How comfortable or confident would you be talking about spiritual matters with colleagues and pupils?
- Take some time to read your school's mission statement. Are there any examples where you have seen this in action? Or where you have seen it disregarded? How does it apply to you in practical terms, and how you do your job?

Prayer

Disturb us, Lord, when
we are too well pleased with ourselves,
when our dreams have come true
because we have dreamed too little,
when we arrive safely
because we sail too close to the shore.
Disturb us, Lord, to dare more boldly,
to venture on wider seas
where storms will show your mastery;
where losing sight of land,
we shall find stars.

Sir Francis Drake

The teacher does not write on inanimate material, but on the very spirits of human beings.

The Catholic School on the Threshold of the Third Millennium, 19

CHAPTER 5

Is there any difference in the teaching curriculum in a Catholic school?

The answer is "yes" and "no".

In England, Wales and Northern Ireland, Catholic teaching is set within the context of the National Curriculum. Every Catholic school ought to have a radical, faith-based agenda. So in this chapter we will look at whether there is any tension between this and the National Curriculum, and how it is possible to work within the legal framework and provide an education that is both academically first-class and rich in faith.

What are the parameters of the National Curriculum?

The National Curriculum was introduced in all state schools in England, Wales and Northern Ireland in 1988, to ensure that each pupil is given the same standard of education. Not so long ago it wasn't uncommon to hear teachers bemoaning the fact that the National Curriculum was extremely prescriptive, allowing very little room for manoeuvre or creative freedom. In general, however, faith schools, independent and private schools have always been less restricted in respect of the teaching curriculum, while the introduction of academies in recent years has given all schools greater freedom. In Scotland the curriculum is non-statutory, and so is not dictated by the government. It is the responsibility of government to provide the framework for learning and teaching, and responsibility for what is taught rests with local authorities and schools, taking national guidelines and advice into account.

For all these differences, the National Curriculum broadly follows the same pattern and covers a similar range of subjects in all schools in the UK. The key difference is found in the way in which all learning in a Catholic school is set within the beliefs and values of the Catholic Church. While all schools must make some provision for religious education, according to the directives from the bishops, in a Catholic school religious education must occupy at least ten per cent of the teaching time. In addition, the bishops give broad outlines of what content must be included in the RE curriculum.

So, as you can see, religious education in a Catholic school must be at the core of the core curriculum, the lead area of learning – because it is why the school is there in the first place. RE is not just one subject among many, but the foundation of the entire educational process.

The first entitlement of every child

You might be surprised to learn that the 1988 Education Reform Act put spirituality on the teaching agenda for all schools in England, Wales

and Northern Ireland. It states that every child is entitled to be taught a curriculum which:

(a) promotes the spiritual, moral, cultural, mental and physical development of pupils at the school; and

(b) prepares pupils for the opportunities, responsibilities and experiences of adult life.

This is a real challenge for many schools as they struggle to understand what spiritual education is and its relationship with moral, social and cultural values. But Catholic schools have long provided such an education. For example, teachers in Catholic schools are required to clearly identify in their planning how Catholic teaching is going to inform learning.

You might ask, *"Isn't that a bit contrived – like forcing God into everything?"* – but in fact God is already there. What an educator in a Catholic school is attempting to do is illustrate how God is at work in the world through science, history, geography, art, music, physical education – in fact, all learning. In a school that does not have a faith context, these links are not made.

What is SMSC?

Spiritual, moral, social and cultural (SMSC) education is the term that educators use to describe the broader dimension of education, and acknowledge responsibility for far more in a young person's life than a prescribed National Curriculum. Far from being confined to religious education, SMSC encompasses all aspects of learning, including extracurricular and out-of-school activities.

There are four main components of SMSC:

Spiritual education

What people believe about the big questions on the meaning and purpose of life. It is everything about our existence on this planet that really matters. (For more about this, see Chapter 4, "Catholic Spirituality and Ethos".)

Moral education

A pupil's moral development involves acquiring the knowledge, skills, qualities and attitudes they need to make responsible moral decisions and act on them.

Social education

How people relate to self and others, which is influenced by spirituality and their moral code.

Cultural education

The ways in which people do things – the rites, rituals, customs and practices that develop over time within communities. (For more about this in the context of a Catholic school, see Chapter 8.) Culture gives expression to a community's spirituality, morality and social values; this is telling and celebrating the story of who we are.

Does this mean that academic achievement comes second in a Catholic school?

Absolutely not! Far from diluting academic teaching, the Catholic ethos and sense of purpose should make teaching truly multi-dimensional, filling it with a heightened sense of wonder and curiosity.

Not only that, but as we saw in Chapter 3, Catholic schools consistently outperform national averages. A Catholic school is accountable to the local bishop, who must ensure that academic standards are high. This has been the case since long before Ofsted, and goes back to the Canon Law of the Catholic Church:

> *Directors of Catholic schools are to take care... that the instruction which is given in them is at least as academically distinguished as that in the other schools of the area.*
>
> Canon 806, §2

The government rightly calls for every school to be at least "good". The Catholic Church goes further, and requires that they are "distinguished".

In educating the whole person, a Catholic school strives to ensure excellence for all. But as well as academic excellence, learning is situated within

RUGBY

the context of Christian beliefs and values, because all learning is seen as interconnected. One area informs another and helps to make sense of some of the questions raised. A good Catholic school makes those connections so that the pupils can learn about and from a subject, but also see *why* they are studying it.

So how do the Catholic agenda and the National Curriculum sit side by side?

They don't! The beliefs and values of the Catholic Church should provide the context for and substantially shape how the National Curriculum is applied and taught in a Catholic school. Critical thinking is at the heart of learning – and this view is deeply held among Catholic educators. It leads to deep learning, which is the opposite of rote learning, and encourages questioning, personal growth and wisdom. Across the taught curriculum, teachers in Catholic schools strive to ensure that the big questions concerning the purpose and meaning of life are raised and faced. Often there are no simple answers, but the important thing is to engage with and explore these issues with questioning minds and honest hearts. In this way the teacher ends up with a radical, exciting and challenging curriculum in which questioning, intellectual curiosity and critical thinking are encouraged.

It's important to emphasise that this does not mean that there are not very good schools, teachers and educators working in other types of school. But the difference, as we have seen in previous chapters, is that the beliefs and values of the Christian faith, spirituality and ethos underpin *everything* and should influence every aspect of a Catholic school.

Are we singing from the same song sheet in teaching the National Curriculum?

Most teachers in Catholic schools will inevitably have to face dilemmas from time to time about how to deliver the National Curriculum. For example, in Science Key Stage 1 there is a section which deals with life and living processes entitled: "Animals, including humans". Students are asked to:

- Notice that animals, including humans, have offspring which grow into adults.
- Find out about and describe the basic needs of animals, including humans, for survival (water, food and air).
- Describe the importance for humans of exercise, eating the right amounts of different types of food, and hygiene.

From a scientific perspective this looks fine. In Catholic teaching, however, every human being is made in the image of God, thus all human life is sacred, and human beings are the highest form of life. So as a teacher in a Catholic school this raises a question as to whether this is the right starting point for such an important topic. This is not about forcing a certain, fixed viewpoint on anyone, so much as questioning the assumption that humans are only animals.

As we shall see from the examples* in the next section, if pupils are encouraged to explore the issues fully for themselves using their critical thinking skills, they will reach their own conclusions in their own way – which is what we want. And there's nothing wrong with pointing out a possible discrepancy between assumptions in the National Curriculum and Catholic teaching, and making that an important talking point.

* While recognising that there is a new National Curriculum from 2014, the examples provided over the page can still be used as guides to good practice.

How does this look at secondary level, from the teacher's and student's point of view?

Science Key Stage 4, Years 10 and 11
Topic: Genetics

The National Curriculum requires schools to teach the subject of genetics: characteristics and variation; genes and chromosomes; cell division; sexual and asexual reproduction; genetic inheritance; genetic diseases; DNA; mutations; genetic engineering; cloning; evolution and natural selection. In response, one Catholic school has set this material within a context that links science and Catholic beliefs and values as part of the learning. This is an extract from a subject leader's medium-term plans:

The Genetics topic at Key Stage 4 allows the science department to explore the spiritual and moral issues associated with cloning animals, the human genome project, and "designer babies"... Year 10 students focus on the tensions that arise from scientific knowledge, power and moral conscience.

So, for example, Year 10 students study "the exploration and study of... the tensions between scientific knowledge, power and moral conscience", while Year 11 look at "current issues such as cloning animals and genetically modified foodstuffs and potential future advancements such as the creation of 'designer babies'". They also "explore the moral issues raised to feed into a bioethics debate on science, knowledge, power and moral conscience".

Here is feedback from a student:

To say that our talents are our own doing is to misjudge our place in creation and to mistake our role with God's. If bioengineering made the myth of the "self-made man" a fact, it would be difficult to see our talents as gifts from God for which we are indebted. This is difficult to accept.

Lisa, Year 11

Geography Key Stage 3, Year 8
Topic: Industry

The National Curriculum requires schools to provide opportunities for pupils to:

- Build on and expand their personal experiences of geography.
- Explore real and relevant contemporary contexts.
- Participate in informed responsible action in relation to geographical issues that affect them and those around them.
- Examine geographical issues in the news.
- Make links between geography and other subjects, including citizenship and ICT, and areas of the curriculum including sustainability and global dimension.

Again, the subject leader has responded by setting this within the context of Catholic beliefs and values, with an emphasis on social justice. These topics are from medium-term planning:

- Promotion of the common good and economic justice.
- Sweatshops – profit being the main aim.
- Can we ever change people's appetite for feeding their desires rather than their needs?
- Am I my neighbour's keeper?

Here is what Year 8 student Marie had to say about it:

Worse than the hours and conditions is the mindset that gives rise to sweatshops. It is a mentality that places profit above human lives. Our worth is no longer tied to our God-given human dignity, but to economic capacity. We have a duty to challenge this train of thought.

In the examples on the left, we look at the National Curriculum at Key Stages 3 and 4, and see how teachers have situated the learning within a Catholic context in their medium-term planning.

Other feedback from students shows how imbuing education with Catholic beliefs and values can lead students to think deeply about the big questions and their own unique place in the story of humankind. For example, Karen, a Year 11 student studying the topic of ratio and proportion in mathematics Key Stage 4, said of what she had learnt:

This topic has really helped me to see both the harmony and diversity in God's beautiful world.

Year 9 student Tom studied the English topic "Voice of the voiceless – the power of the poet":

The most powerful poem for me is WH Auden's "Refugee Blues". It is really challenging because Auden shows how easy it can be to reduce people who are different to being less than animals. Reading the poem makes you feel it. He really makes you think about what it is to be a human being and the sacredness of life.

These are powerful testimonies to the importance of teaching young people to think deeply and find answers for themselves. Based on its deeply held principles of social justice, this is the kind of teaching that the Catholic Church encourages and promotes. For many in a teaching role it is an experience both thrilling and humbling – and a mission both daunting and magnificent.

The tribute to Caesar

As we have seen, governors and headteachers face considerable challenges in running a faith school within a secular education system – and it would be dishonest to pretend otherwise. But not only is it possible to meet these challenges head on, it is also rewarding and fulfilling. The brilliant story in Matthew 22:17-21 shows us how Jesus responds to the challenge.

To set the story in context, Jesus is in Jerusalem, speaking to a (largely) Jewish crowd. At that time, Jerusalem was under Roman rule, with the Roman ruler, or Caesar, demanding taxes from the Jews. Not only did they resent the financial burden, but it was a religious affront even to have to touch coins bearing the image of Caesar, who claimed to be a god. The Pharisees were the respected teachers among the Jews, known for their strict interpretation of the Law. You meet them sometimes in the Gospels confronting Jesus on a variety of issues, and Jesus always responds with honesty and wisdom. In this passage, the Pharisees ask Jesus for his response:

"Give us your opinion, then. Is it permissible to pay taxes to Caesar or not?"

How to answer, that is the challenge. If Jesus answers "no", he is in trouble for encouraging people to break the law by not paying their taxes. On the other hand, if he says "yes", he will infuriate his Jewish listeners by appearing to side with the detested Roman authorities:

But Jesus was aware of their malice and replied, "You hypocrites! Why are you putting me to the test? Show me the money you pay the tax with." They handed him a denarius [a Roman coin], and he said, "Whose portrait is this? Whose title?" They replied, "Caesar's". Then he said to them, "Very well, pay Caesar what belongs to Caesar – and God what belongs to God."

Note that Jesus asks to be shown the coin but does not touch it. Then he sidesteps the Pharisees' trap. Taxes, he says, must be paid to Caesar, but give only the tax and nothing more... You belong to God.

Catholic schools may sometimes feel obliged to adopt or respond to prevailing cultural beliefs and values. And while Catholic educationalists know and acknowledge that young people need to be prepared for the real world, the Catholic school is driven by beliefs, values and a spirituality that takes it far beyond prevailing cultural trends or any government agenda through its shared vision and values.

How do I find out more about Catholic teaching?

Scripture

If you work in a teaching role, it's a really good idea to read up on Catholic teaching, and scripture – the seventy-three books which make up the two sections of the Bible (Old Testament and New) – is the best place to start, not least because it is the

inspired word of God. It is definitely a good idea to own a Bible, and to turn to it when you want answers to questions – your own or someone else's. It may be bewildering at first, but soon you will start to find your way around it. More than that, it's a good idea to sit quietly with it – if possible every day – and to familiarise yourself with this extraordinary book. It is the most-read book ever. For many people, Christian and non-Christian, the Bible is a source of wisdom, understanding, history, morality and spiritual strength – your single most valuable resource.

Tradition and the Magisterium

Church teaching is also found in a variety of other sources, such as "tradition". Coming from the Latin word *tradere* meaning "to hand on", tradition in this context has a specific meaning, and refers to what the disciples taught the early Christian communities. This oral teaching lasted for some time, and it was not until Jesus' first disciples died that the written word came into existence and the books of the New Testament started to be written:

So then, brothers and sisters, stand firm and hold to the traditions that you were taught by us, either by word of mouth or by our letter.

2 Thessalonians 2:15

The word *magisterium* comes from the Latin *magister*, meaning "teacher", and refers to the teaching role of the Church, most usually exercised by the pope and the bishops. This is based on the promise Christ made to his disciples when he sent them out on mission: "Whoever listens to you listens to me, and whoever rejects you rejects me, and whoever rejects me rejects the one who sent me" (Luke 10:16). When the Church presents a doctrine as definitive or final, it is considered to be without error.

All those things are to be believed by divine and Catholic faith which are contained in the written Word of God or in Tradition, and which are proposed by the Church, either in solemn judgment or in its ordinary and universal teaching office, as divinely revealed truths which must be believed.

First Vatican Council, 1870

The Catechism of the Catholic Church

This is a written summary of Christian teaching. It was first published in French in 1992, followed by many other languages. You might find it difficult to read if you are not used to church language, especially if you are trying to answer those challenging questions that students tend to ask. However, a really useful place to start is *Youcat*[1] – a simplified version, co-written by Pope Benedict XVI, which has become a world bestseller since its publication in 2011. It is intended for young people, but in it you will find useful summaries of the key teachings of the Church.

Do Catholic schools deal with the controversial issues of today?

You may have heard all sorts of odd opinions about what is or isn't taught in a Catholic school, but the reality is that a Catholic school strives to prepare its young people for the world just as they will meet it, to enable them to engage with real life. A good school encourages questioning and higher-

[1] *Youcat: The Youth Catechism of the Catholic Church* (London: Catholic Truth Society. 2011).

order thinking from nursery through to the sixth form and beyond. Here are some commonly held myths about Catholic teaching:

Myth 1 – Students are "force-fed" religion in a Catholic school

Believe it or not, the idea that religious education is forced on students without question is still prevalent. This could not be further from the truth. In reality you will find that most RE lessons are thought-provoking and designed to encourage real exploration. Faith is a gift from God – and those who have it can share that gift with others. Pupils are encouraged to explore and seek real truth so that, hopefully, they will grow in their own understanding and wisdom.

Myth 2 – All Catholics believe in creationism

People often ask with incredulity, "Do you really believe that the world was created in seven days?" This is also something that frequently arises with younger children who want to know about Adam and Eve and dinosaurs, and how they all fit together. A creationist takes the account of creation in the book of Genesis chapter one literally, and holds that the world was created by God in seven days. On the other hand, a Darwinist (and most scientists) believe that the world evolved over millions of years from a yet-undefined first cause. At the end of the day, Catholics don't want to pit science against religion – they want science to inform religion and vice versa. Catholics do emphatically believe that God created the world, but are not required to see the first chapter of Genesis as a scientific document, but a myth intended to tell the truth of the matter – that a loving God created the world.

Myth 3 – All sex is sinful

In a Catholic school, sex education is set within the context of personal, social and health education (PSHE), and provided as part of the curriculum. It is also situated within the beliefs and values of the Catholic Church, which teaches that sex is a gift from God, a beautiful expression of love and the sacred. For many people, the media and commerce exploit the human person in their relentless marketing of sex – often for selfish gratification, disassociated from a loving permanent relationship – and this has a negative impact on society and our respect for sex and sexuality. The Church aspires to the highest possible respect for the human person as made in the image and likeness of God. Therefore, it will speak out strongly against anything that uses, abuses or devalues a person's dignity.

Myth 4 – Catholic schools are divisive

"Catholic" means "one", "universal" – so a Catholic school, by definition, is uniting and inclusive rather than divisive. But, of course, that has to be put into practice. Despite being set up to offer Catholic education for Catholic children (which is its entitlement under the law of the land), as we saw in Chapter 3, Catholic schools are statistically more diverse than national averages. But this is about much more than statistics – it's about the Church wanting to be truly universal, and following Jesus' example of reaching people of all backgrounds, wherever they are in the world.

Myth 5 – Catholicism is obsessed with sin and guilt

The cliché that Catholics are guilt-ridden and sin-obsessed certainly was true in the past. You don't hear as much these days about guilt, thankfully, but sin is a reality which needs to be understood by anybody who works in a Catholic school. Perhaps the best place to go for a definition is *Youcat* (see section on the Catechism on page 47), which says that sin is a "rejection of God and the refusal to accept his love". The same can be said for hell, which again seemed to take up a lot of Catholic thinking in the past. No one has said that hell doesn't exist any more. Again, *Youcat* is very helpful when it defines hell as a state of separation from God that a person has wished for himself or herself after death even when faced with the love and mercy of God. It is interesting to note that the Catholic Church has never named any human being as being in hell, even though there are more than a few strong candidates throughout history!

POINTS TO REMEMBER

- You are not expected to have all the answers.
- There is no area or issue that you can't raise and explore.

POINTS FOR PERSONAL REFLECTION OR GROUP DISCUSSION

- Has any part of this chapter challenged you as a member of staff – if so, why?
- Do you feel you need further support in developing your understanding of SMSC education in a Catholic school?
- Would you agree that setting learning within the context of Catholic beliefs and values brings it alive?

TOP TIPS

- Identify your needs and don't be afraid to ask for the necessary training.
- Identify the key people in school who can help you.
- Make a "big question book" to record questions you are asked and are not sure how to answer, so you can explore them for yourself and respond to students' questions.

Reflection

Dear Teacher:

I am a survivor of a concentration camp.
My eyes saw what no man should witness:
gas chambers built by learned engineers;
children poisoned by educated physicians;
infants killed by trained nurses;
women and babies shot and burned by high school and college graduates.
So I am suspicious of education.
My request is: help your students become more human.
Your efforts must never produce learned monsters, skilled psychopaths, educated Eichmanns.
Reading, writing, and arithmetic are important only if they serve to make our children more humane.[2]

[2] Letter from a Holocaust survivor to educators, published in Haim Ginott, *Teacher and Child: A Book for Parents and Teachers,* p. 317 (New York: Scribner, 1993).

CHAPTER 6

Catholic social teaching

People today – arguably more than ever – are desperate to know how to respond to the problems of the world – war and disaster, injustice, poverty. What's more, big business and the nation state are apparently oblivious to, or wilfully ignore, the damage they are doing to the environment.

Our young people in particular are hungry to feel heard and needed. Most of them really want to make a difference and feel that their existence matters. In addition, they are usually very clear and insightful about what constitutes injustice, and want to be supported and encouraged to bring about a fairer society and to be better stewards of the environment, which is God's creation.

The Church's response to the world's pain

There is a body of teaching in the Catholic Church, which is just about as challenging as it can get. Most people have little or no knowledge of it, yet it often ignites real interest and passion, especially in the young. It is known as Catholic social teaching – nicknamed "our best-kept secret". Why is this? Well, because it is truly radical, very challenging and, for some, disturbing.

Catholic social teaching stems from the "Great Commandment" to put God first and to love your brother and sister as yourself and to act as if what happens to them also happens to you.

"Teacher, which commandment in the law is the greatest?" He said to him, "'You shall love the Lord your God with all your heart, and with all your soul, and with all your mind.' This is the greatest and first commandment. And a second is like it: 'You shall love your neighbour as yourself.' On these two commandments hang all the law and the prophets."

Matthew 22:36-40

The issues covered in the Church's social teaching can be broadly categorised into the following themes:

- Human dignity
- The option for the poor
- The dignity of work
- Solidarity
- Catholic teaching on poverty: a place at the table
- Faithful citizenship: a call to political responsibility
- Social justice
- Human and economic development
- On social sin

Makuu in the school vegetable garden in a project funded by CAFOD in Kenya which aims to bring nutrition to pupils through vegetables and to teach them how to grow crops.

In 2012, Benedict XVI's New Year message addressed the need to educate young people in the urgent issues of justice and peace. He addressed all those responsible for educating and forming young people, pointing out that real education is "in truth and freedom" (*Educating Young People in Justice and Peace*, 3), the source of which is God. Young people, he said, must be educated in justice because this is at the very heart of who we are as human beings. We must see this as being in solidarity and love for all people. Peace, he said, is both a divine gift and a human task and responsibility:

With his election, Pope Francis – who, as he himself said, came "from the ends of the earth" – picked up this theme. In his first week as pope, he spoke of the need for the Church to be seen as "poor and for the poor". In taking the name Francis, after St Francis of Assisi, he was paying tribute to someone who had been totally dedicated to serving the poor and marginalised. It was seen by many as another indication that the Church is making it an urgent priority to respond to the cry of the poor wherever they are found.

Where did it start?

Based on God's revelation in Christ, the Church has been developing its body of social teaching as long as it has existed. Catholic social teaching first began to be formulated as a system in the late nineteenth century. Pope Leo XIII is credited with having introduced it in 1891 with his encyclical *Rerum Novarum*. Successive popes have added to and developed it, principally in the form of encyclicals (letters). These have Latin titles – but don't let that put you off. They are all translated into accessible English. The quickest way to find the texts is to go online and type in the title. The Vatican website is a very good place to start (**www.vatican.va**).

In order to be true peacemakers, we must educate ourselves in compassion, solidarity, working together, fraternity, in being active within the community and concerned to raise awareness about national and international issues and the importance of seeking adequate mechanisms for the redistribution of wealth, the promotion of growth, cooperation for development and conflict resolution.

Educating Young People in Justice and Peace, 5

There you will find:

- *Rerum Novarum* (On the Condition of Labour) – Pope Leo XIII, 1891
- *Quadragesimo Anno* (After Forty Years) – Pope Pius XI, 1931
- *Mater et Magistra* (Christianity and Social Progress) – Pope John XXIII, 1961
- *Pacem in Terris* (Peace on Earth) – Pope John XXIII, 1963
- *Gaudium et Spes* (Pastoral Constitution on the Church in the Modern World) – Vatican Council II, 1965
- *Populorum Progressio* (On the Development of Peoples) – Pope Paul VI, 1967
- *Octogesima Adveniens* (A Call to Action) – Pope Paul VI, 1971
- *Justicia in Mundo* (Justice in the World) – Synod of Bishops, 1971
- *Laborem Exercens* (On Human Work) – Pope John Paul II, 1981
- *Sollicitudo Rei Socialis* (On Social Concern) – Pope John Paul II, 1987
- *Centesimus Annus* (The Hundredth Year) – Pope John Paul II, 1991
- *Evangelium Vitae* (The Gospel of Life) – Pope John Paul II, 1995
- *Fides et Ratio* (Faith and Reason) – Pope John Paul II, 1998
- *Deus Caritas Est* (God Is Love) – Benedict XVI, 2005
- *Sacramentum Caritatis* (Apostolic Exhortation on the Eucharist) – Benedict XVI, 2007
- *Caritas in Veritate* (Charity in Truth) – Benedict XVI, 2009

As these documents show, Catholic social teaching concerns just about everything that needs to be put right and transformed, to enable the beauty and dignity of all people to shine. Take a look at some of these quotations from church documents. Pay attention to how challenging and radical they are – not what you might expect from the Church. But they all inform the teaching in a Catholic school, particularly under the headings of spiritual, moral, social and cultural education (SMSC – see page 40):

"Each generation takes the natural environment on loan, and must return it after use in as good or better condition as when it was first borrowed."

"[On the media] It is always easier to drive taste… downwards."

"State welfare provision [is not] a desirable substitute for payment of a just wage."

"The defeat of Communism should not mean the triumph of unbridled capitalism."

"The nation's real crisis is not economic, but moral and spiritual."

"We believe that it is in the growing priority of technology over ethics, in the growing primacy of things over persons, and in the growing superiority of matter over spirit, that the most serious threats to British society now lie."

The Bishops of England and Wales, *The Common Good*, 14

"Excessive economic and social inequalities within the one human family, between individuals and between peoples, give rise to scandal and are contrary to social justice, to equity, and to the dignity of the human person, as well as to peace within society and at the international level."

Pastoral Constitution on the Church in the Modern World, 29, as cited in *The Common Good*

"In his desire to have and to enjoy rather than to be and to grow, man consumes the resources of the earth and his own life in an excessive and disordered way."

Pope John Paul II, The Hundredth Year, 37, as cited in *The Common Good*

What are the principles of Catholic social teaching?

Catholics believe that "humanity is one family despite differences of nationality or race".[1] This is at the heart of Catholic social teaching, and means that:

- We all make up the people of God – there are no outsiders!
- We are all part of the Body of Christ – there are no dismembered bits!
- We are called to live in communion – as one – with ourselves, each other and God.

The preferential option for the poor

People who are poor and vulnerable have a special place in Catholic social teaching: this is what is meant by the "preferential option for the poor".

The poor are not a burden; they are our brothers and sisters. Christ taught us that our neighbourhood is universal: so loving our neighbour has global dimensions... Solidarity with our neighbour is also about the promotion of equality of rights and equality of opportunities; hence we must oppose all forms of discrimination and racism.

Bishops of England and Wales, *The Common Good*, 14

With this comes considerable responsibility for the choices we make – to act or not to act. We are all accountable:

The joys and hopes, the grief and anguish of the people of our time, especially of those who are poor or afflicted, are the joys and hopes, the grief and anguish of the followers of Christ.

Pastoral Constitution on the Church in the Modern World

Scripture tells us that every human being is made in the image of God, so each individual is the clearest reflection of God among us. Accordingly, the Catholic social vision has as its focal point the human person – whatever their social status, demographic, background, ethnicity, attractiveness, education:

Christ challenges us to see his presence in our neighbour, especially the neighbour who suffers or who lacks what is essential to human flourishing.

Bishops of England and Wales, *The Common Good*, 12

Catholic social teaching in the daily life of the school

The social teaching of the Church is a response to people's longing to answer the cry of the poor and marginalised, and Catholic education seeks to offer young people something worth committing to – a faith that is lived in action for justice. The key word here is "action". *The principle of Catholic social teaching is that from a "living faith" comes "loving action", which brings about transformation into a "civilization of love".*[2] The task of educators (in the widest possible sense of the word) is to enable and encourage those they are educating to bring about change where it is needed. This can be a challenging process, involving self-sacrifice, humility and letting go of our fixed ideas about ourselves and one another – but it must be demonstrated by our actions.

Catholic schools are very keen to be actively engaged in action for social justice. In harnessing young people's enthusiasm, drive and energy, they usually excel in both the scope of what they undertake and the results – for example, fundraising

[1] The Bishops of England and Wales, 1996, *The Common Good*, 14. Accessed at **www.catholicsocialteaching.org.uk**, 21/03/13.
[2] Michael J. Schultheis: *Our Best Kept Secret: The Rich Heritage of Catholic Social Teaching*, p. 6 (London: CAFOD, 1988).
See also Compendium of the Social Doctrine of the Church. Accessed at **http://www.vatican.va/roman_curia/pontifical_councils/justpeace/documents/rc_pc_justpeace_doc_20060526_compendio-dott-soc_en.html**, 21/03/13.

and charitable activities. There are many charities willing and able to support schools in promoting Catholic social teaching – their aim is to ensure that it is a lived reality rather than a taught theory. You will find some of these charities listed at the back of the book.

Within the teaching curriculum, the most obvious area for Catholic social teaching is of course religious teaching. But it is all-pervasive and touches on every aspect of life, so equally significant across all areas of teaching and learning. The spiritual, moral, social and cultural curriculum supports and extends what is taught in RE. For example, the topic of "human dignity" crosses into many subject areas. Think about the dignity of the body seen from the perspective of science, art, PE, literature – to mention just a few. Again, think about poverty, social sin, work, and human and economic development within the context of history and geography. Teachers and classroom assistants often have difficulty in narrowing the field to make it manageable in a lesson. So there is quite a planning challenge here – but a very worthwhile one.

As we have seen in other chapters, every member of staff in a Catholic school is in some way teaching. Whether you are the headteacher or receptionist, just by being who you are, you are showing students and staff an example of humanity – whether you are generous-hearted or mean-spirited, compassionate or uncaring, engaged with the life of the school or at one remove from it. So, Catholic social teaching, which is all about generosity, compassion and being "switched on" to one another, affects each and every one of us, just as we affect everyone we come into contact with. In a Catholic school, you should be able to discern Catholic social teaching

in action everywhere – in the relationships (even when they are challenging), policies, ethos and atmosphere of the place. If it is not there, or there are gaps, it is your place and – yes – your responsibility to challenge it and encourage the school and individuals within it to get back to the principles of Catholic social teaching.

You must be the change you want to see in the world.

Mahatma Gandhi, leader of the Indian nationalist movement against British rule

POINTS FOR PERSONAL REFLECTION OR GROUP DISCUSSION

- What has challenged you in this chapter, and why?
- Young people are often idealistic. To what extent do you think the school can foster their understanding of the complexities within issues of justice and peace?
- Read the prayer of St Teresa on this page. What are your thoughts and feelings about what she says? In what way, if any, is it true for you?

TOP TIPS

- Focus on what you can do well and do it better.
- Engage an outside specialist if you feel unsure about anything. Many agencies will give their time and expertise for free.

Reflection

CHRIST HAS NO BODY

Christ has no body now but yours
No hands, no feet on earth but yours
Yours are the eyes through which he looks
Compassion on this world
Yours are the feet with which he walks to do good
Yours are the hands with which he blesses all the world
Yours are the hands
Yours are the feet
Yours are the eyes
You are his body
Christ has no body now on earth but yours.

St Teresa of Avila

THE HOPES OF THIS COMMUNITY

The hopes of this community cannot be overcome.
They are a thousand branches of blossom, flowering with freedom.
Life will come.

Brother, you have brought life to our home
and you live the Word of the one who is the truth.
May you drink our wine and share our bread
amidst people of solidarity who want to go forward.

Sister, you have brought stars to our home.
Harvests of smiles begin to break out.
May we give praise to him who, on the journey,
was life and the Word for a people in freedom.

Perhaps the new time has not yet come
and you feel that your eyes are full of darkness.
Hold your people tight and walk with them.
His life and his Word will be your dawn.

CAFOD Precoma, Colombia

CHAPTER 7

Meet the family

One big family?

You may hear the language of the family used a lot in your school – or it should be – because in a Catholic school you find the family of the Church, or at least a branch of the family tree.

The Church takes its family language all the way back to its teaching of God as our Father and Jesus as his Son. Jesus emphasised this relationship when he referred to God as "Abba" (Mark 14:36) – a term of affection which translates as something like "Dad".

What's more, we believe we are called to be brothers and sisters – to Jesus (see Matthew 12:50) and to one another. St Paul certainly thought so, and in his letters to the men and women of the early Church, he frequently addresses his readers as "brothers and sisters" (for example, in Romans 16:17). This is why clergy and religious are known as "Brother", "Sister" or "Father".

The People of God

The Church is first and foremost people, gathered under Christ, the head of the Church. While it is also an institution, it is primarily a community. An important principle adopted by the Second Vatican Council is embodied in its teaching that the Church is the whole *People of God* (see the *Dogmatic Constitution of the Church*, chapter 2). In other words, the Church is not only the hierarchy, the clergy, and members of religious communities, but the whole community of the baptised.

Like any family, the Church organises itself into roles, and in this section we will look at some of the people who make up the People of God – the laity, the clergy, and the men and women in religious orders – and the roles they play. You are likely to see some of them regularly in the school, while others will visit on special occasions. In Appendix 1 (on page 76) you will find a practical guide on how to address them if you are introduced, or making a formal introduction, or corresponding with them.

The laity

The overwhelming majority of Catholics are lay people. "Lay" simply distinguishes them from clergy (e.g. priests) or religious (e.g. nuns). All (lay, clergy, religious) work together for the glory of God and all are valued, active participants in the life of the Church.

A lay chaplain

In some parts of the country, parishes have been amalgamated and it is not possible for one priest to be in school as much as he may wish – or your parish may be very large and the parish priest can't be in school as often as you would like. Therefore, a qualified and suitable lay person is appointed as a lay chaplain to the

school. This has to be done with the full backing of the governors and the bishop.

Members of religious orders

A member of a religious order is often simply referred to as "a religious". The terms "monk" and "nun" refer to members of enclosed religious orders, while members of orders which are not enclosed are usually referred to as religious sisters or religious brothers. A "novice" is someone who has been accepted into a religious order and who is undergoing a period of training and formation (or "novitiate") before taking any vows. Typically these vows are poverty, chastity and obedience.

Religious orders divide into three main types:

- Apostolic: meaning they are founded to work in the world and, although they have a very clear commitment to a life of prayer, their key function is to serve God through caring for others.

- Monastic: those who live in monasteries. They too do great work helping the poor and in the field of education, but they generally tend to be based in their monasteries.

- Contemplative: whose main vocation is to pray for the world. They live in religious houses or monasteries. You could describe them as the great prayer powerhouses of the Church.

A deacon

There are two types of deacon. One is the "transitional" deacon – someone who has been ordained as a deacon as the final stage of preparation to be ordained as a priest (they normally remain a deacon for about a year). The other type is the "permanent" deacon, ordained by the bishop to that role, who will remain a deacon and not be ordained a priest – they are often older, married men. The latter are to be found in many parishes now, and so are probably more likely to be encountered in school. They are able to do a great deal, except celebrate Mass or the sacrament of reconciliation – sacraments which are only administered by ordained priests (see Chapter 8).

A parish priest

He is appointed by the bishop to your parish, and his main duties are preaching, celebrating Mass, administering the other sacraments and exercising a role of leadership within the Church. You will certainly meet your parish priest in school, as well as at many other events in the community life of the parish. The parish priest is usually on the school's governing body, and is often also the chaplain to the school. He has responsibility for looking after the geographical area known as the parish, which is the "grass roots" of the life of the Church.

A canon

Every cathedral has a group of priests appointed by the bishop to form the "chapter" – or governing body – of the cathedral. This chapter has responsibility for running the cathedral and assisting the bishop in his decision-making. In some dioceses a canon may well be responsible for the running of the education department, ensuring that the diocesan policies are in place across all schools and keeping the bishop fully informed. You may well meet him if you visit the cathedral with the school, or at an important event in the life of the school. Canons often have other responsibilities in the diocese, sometimes for education, or finances, or a particular area of pastoral responsibility. For some, "canon" is simply an honorary title, not belonging to the chapter.

A vicar general (or monsignor)

These are priests who are appointed to assist in the running of the diocese. They often have other responsibilities as well, so again you may well meet them. Although a vicar general will usually be a monsignor, not all monsignors are vicars general.

A bishop

The bishop is appointed directly by the pope. He is responsible for the running of a diocese and has full authority within his own diocese. You may see him quite often.

An archbishop

The archbishop has the same authority as any bishop. He is responsible for a large or important diocese known as an "archdiocese".

A cardinal

Cardinals are personally appointed by the pope. Their primary job is to elect the next pope. However, because the Catholic Church has over a billion members, the pope relies on around 120 of his cardinals to help run the Church. Some are stationed in Rome, heading up the departments of the Church. This group is called the Roman Curia. Those not based in Rome lead archdioceses around the world. They have full administrative authority within their areas. You may well meet the cardinal in school for a special occasion or at a national or diocesan gathering.

The pope

The successor of St Peter – head of the worldwide Catholic Church – also known as the Bishop of Rome, or the Servant of the Servants of God. His role is to hold the universal Church together and guide it into the future – not an easy job, you will agree. But he is assisted and helped by the cardinals and bishops across the world. He visits very rarely, but you never know!

The structure of a Catholic school

Who's in charge?

Ultimately it is the bishop of the diocese (see above). He delegates most of his powers to the governors. He appoints the majority of governors, and these are known as "foundation governors" (see below). The governing body then delegates the day-to-day running of the school to the headteacher. The chair of the governing body and the headteacher work closely together to ensure the school and its teachings remain authentically Catholic.

Who teaches?

The lead teacher is the headteacher, who must be a practising Catholic, ready and able to witness to the teachings of the Gospel and Church. The head has the difficult task of having to balance the government's agenda and the agenda of the Church. Sometimes the two clash and that can be very tricky for the school's leadership.

In addition, all those in key positions, such as the deputy head and the head of department for religious education, or RE co-ordinator, must be practising Catholics. Other than that, there may be many teachers and staff members who are not Catholic. What is important is that everyone knows and understands the school mission statement and aims and objectives, and feels able to support them and encourage others to live them out.

What do governors do?

Governors are our unsung heroes – really important people. At the end of the day they are your employer, and are appointed to ensure that the school fulfils its mission

and strives for excellence. To carry out their duties to the best of their ability they need to know as much as possible about the school, and have a clear picture of the quality of teaching and learning so they can support the head. It is not an easy job and it is amazing that so many people are willing to give their time and expertise for free!

The governing body will consist of foundation governors, parent governors, staff governors, and Local Authority governors. As we have seen, foundation governors are appointed by the bishop and have a majority on the governing body. Their role includes a duty to preserve and promote the Catholic nature of the school, as described in the ethos statement and trust deed.

You will meet the governors at big events, as well as in supporting roles from time to time. For example, in primary schools it's not uncommon for a governor with a particular area of expertise to give one-to-one support in areas of the curriculum, under the direction of the class teacher. Some will give their time and skills in a wide variety of activities, such as administration, mealtimes and extracurricular activities.

Jesus – the model of servant leadership

The Gospels contain some very interesting and challenging insights into leadership. When Jesus came to public attention, many people thought that this wonder-worker had come to free Israel from the tyranny of Roman occupation. Jesus was, indeed, the longed-for Messiah, but not in the form of an avenging liberator – as some Jews had expected. Instead, he turned conventional wisdom on its head and redefined leadership in ways we are still trying to come to terms with.

In Mark's Gospel Jesus tells his disciples, "whoever wishes to become great among you must be your servant" (10:43) – something he lived out in his ministry. Here are two more examples from the Bible, of Jesus demonstrating "servant leadership".

Jesus enters Jerusalem (Luke 19:28-40)
This passage tells the story of how Jesus entered Jerusalem. By this point he had huge crowds following him everywhere he went. But he refused to make it a triumphal procession and instead rode on a humble donkey, deliberately making the point that his mission is nothing to do with domination, control or show.

Jesus washes the disciples' feet (John 13:1-17)
In John's account of the Last Supper, Jesus washes the feet of his disciples. It was usually the slave who had the less-than-pleasant job of cleaning guests' feet – it really wasn't something you would volunteer to do. That is why the disciples were so appalled when Jesus did it. What was he playing at? They recoiled at his show of humility but Jesus insisted, in order to teach them something about his kind of leadership.

The servants of the servants of God

Like any community, the Church goes through phases when its foundational beliefs are strong, and other times when they are weaker. There have been times in the life of the Church when the clergy have striven to emulate Jesus' example of servant leadership – and other times when power has gone to people's heads.

Pope Gregory the Great in the late sixth century was the first pope to use the phrase "servant of the servants of God" to remind the bishops of their vocation to serve. He also saw himself in a servant role, and signed his letters "Gregory, Servant of the Servants of God".

In more recent years, particularly since the Second Vatican Council, there has been a fresh move to revive the concept and practice of servant leadership in the Church. Archbishop Vincent Nichols, writing about his student days in Rome during the Second Vatican Council, recalls that in the early days of the Council, the bishops were picked up every morning in limousines. Three years later, they were getting on a coach together to be taken to the Vatican.

The palaces and limos have all but disappeared, and today there is a much more familiar atmosphere around those in the Church who hold high office, without any lessening of respect. When the bishop calls, there is still a sense of excitement,

but in most cases there will not be the same "red carpet" treatment. Not so long ago, it was the tradition to kiss the bishop's ring as a mark of respect. This is less the case now. Most people were amused to see Pope Francis paying his hotel bill after his election (see above).

POINTS TO REMEMBER

- We all have an important role in the family.
- The clergy and religious are here to serve and want to serve. As humans, however, we all fail – so if you find someone falling short of the mark, have the courage to discuss it with them.
- The Church needs you!

POINTS FOR PERSONAL REFLECTION OR GROUP DISCUSSION

- What do you think about the model of servant leadership?
- To what degree, if any, do you feel "part of the family"?
- As a learning community, how do you feel you can grow closer to the family model?

On the other hand, no organisation can exist without a degree of authority or accountability – we would simply be left with a complete free-for-all. Servant leadership is about how this authority is used. Jesus didn't spend his time drawing up rules and regulations, but he spoke with authority (Mark 1:22). It is more to do with truth than the desire to control and dominate. In the Church, we look to the leaders to speak with authority, while at the same time being examples of humble service.

In our schools, we should be looking for much the same thing, although of course the reality is that you will find as many different models of leadership as there are leaders. Some may be clear examples of servant leadership while others… well, let's not be too hard on them! It's not easy being a faith leader in a modern Catholic school – that is why we pray for our leaders!

Getting names and titles right when addressing clergy and religious

Some people are extremely nervous when it comes to addressing or corresponding with clergy and religious. So in Appendix I (on page 76) we have produced a simple guide to help you know how to greet people.

The simple rule is to be formal, both in public and private, unless you are invited to do otherwise. Today many clergy and religious are more comfortable being addressed in a simple fashion on a day-to-day basis, such as "Father", "Brother" or "Sister". However, it is important to know and use the correct protocols in public or before the person in question has expressed their preference. Until then, always stay on the safe side by using the correct terminology.

Prayer

Loving God,
Grant me your hope, that I may know the value of living.
Grant me your strength, that I may have courage whatever happens.
Grant me your patience, that I pause before I judge.
Grant me your wisdom, that I discover how to learn from the children.
Grant me your mercy, that I may temper my discipline.
Grant me your peace, that I may become an instrument of reconciliation.
And in all things flood me in your joy that I may keep alight the flame of your love.
Amen.

CHAPTER 8

Celebrate all year round!

Christians are called to be people of joy and hope, because they know they are loved and have reason to celebrate. The Catholic community loves to celebrate, and opportunities come round regularly. Schools generally do this very well, and observe the seasons and feast days in colour, art, music, liturgy (the Church's official form of worship), assemblies, prayer, and in the classroom.

The Church knows how to teach, and uses signs and symbols, as well as words. But it is important that the liturgical life of the Church is seen as part of a joined-up message, backed up by actions and words.

This chapter deals with the Church's yearly cycle and some of the rites and rituals associated with it. Hopefully it will help you to work out what is happening and, most importantly, how you can contribute. The main thing is to become familiar with the key times of the year, and gain a simple understanding of what they are about. The rest will follow!

Christian celebrations and worship take different forms, including:

- Liturgy: the official prayers and sacraments of the Church.
- Para-liturgy: this is when the school or parish designs its own style of worship in conformity with the liturgy. There is nothing wrong with this, as long as it doesn't replace the liturgy.
- Worship: giving glory, praise and thanks to God.
- Prayer: raising the heart and mind to God, or, simply put, listening and speaking to God. (For more on prayer see page 73.)

The liturgical calendar

The Church's year is made up of seasons, within which are various types of events: commemorations, festivals, feast days and solemnities. A complex set of rules governs which happens when. In addition, some have fixed dates while others can be celebrated on the nearest Sunday. While it may be confusing at first, the result is that no two years will ever look the same – each year has its own unique and colourful pattern of celebration!

While most people celebrate the New Year on 1 January, the Church's yearly cycle begins in late November or early December, starting on the first Sunday in Advent (the fourth Sunday before Christmas day):

THE LITURGICAL YEAR

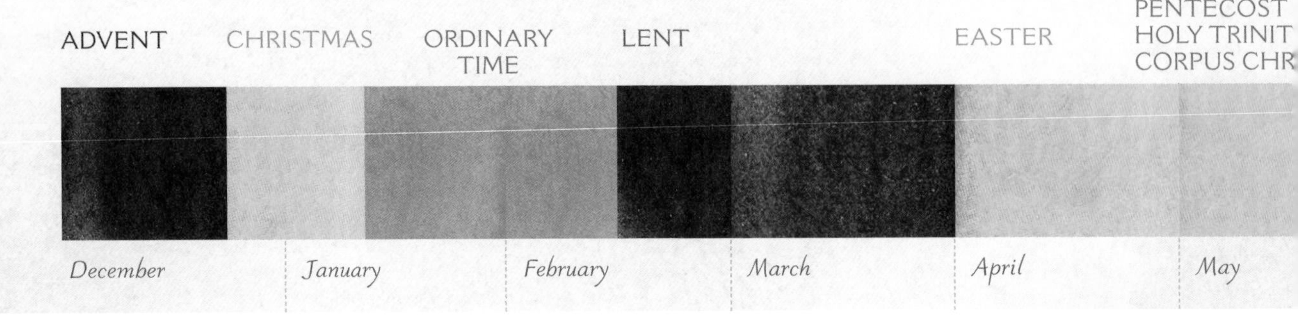

Advent

Liturgical colour: purple
Dates: late November / early December, ending on 24 December

Advent is a season of preparation to meet Christ, both in the celebration of his birth and in his Second Coming. People are sometimes surprised to learn that Advent is a penitential season, one that prepares us to stand ready and be prepared for the Lord's Second Coming. Advent has a strong and positive message. Simply put, the Church is calling us to sort ourselves out. The themes for each week of Advent are: "Wake up!", "Prepare the way of the Lord", "Rejoice", and "Emmanuel is with us". These are sometimes translated as hope, joy, love and peace.

For Catholics, the call to work for charity and the common good is heightened at times like Advent and Lent (see below). It is a time for personal renewal, growth and transformation. God has heard the cry of the poor and comes. Now we must hear this same call to action. Jesus came to save, heal and reconcile – that is a key message of Advent.

Christmas

Liturgical colours: white or gold
Dates: 25 December to the Baptism of the Lord (usually the Sunday after Epiphany)

At Christmas Christians celebrate Immanuel, from the Hebrew for "God with us". That, of course, took place in the form of the birth of Jesus. The Christmas season comes to a close after the feast of the Baptism of the Lord, which is usually held on the Sunday after Epiphany. (Epiphany falls on 6 January and is when Christians celebrate the coming of the magi, or wise men, to worship Jesus.) In some countries, including England, Wales and Scotland, Epiphany is now celebrated on the second Sunday after Christmas. At one time, however, the season lasted for the whole of January and ended with the feast of Candlemas (2 February), which celebrates Jesus being presented in the Temple. So don't be surprised if there are still signs of Christmas when you return to school after the holiday.

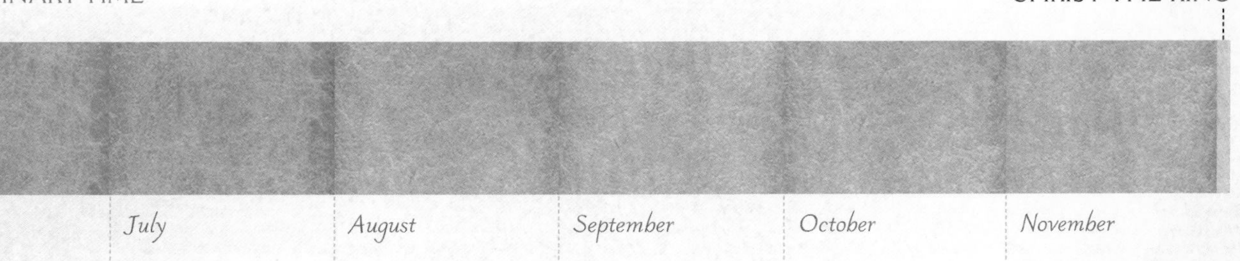

Lent
Liturgical colour: purple
Dates: six weeks between Ash Wednesday and Easter Sunday

Lent reminds Christians of the forty days Jesus spent fasting and praying in the desert before he began his ministry (Matthew 4:1-11). It is when the Church prepares for the greatest of all celebrations – Easter. Because its focus is the lead-up to the death of Jesus, Lent is a serious time when the Church encourages us to pray, fast and abstain, and give alms or do something for the good of the community.

Holy Week is the sixth week of Lent, and forms a dramatic climax to the period. It is when Christians really focus on the events leading up to the crucifixion of Jesus on Good Friday and the resurrection of Jesus on Easter Sunday. Many schools will organise special penitential services, and re-enactments in the form of passion plays or stations of the cross, which represent Jesus' journey to his crucifixion at Calvary.

There are subtle but important variations in the liturgy during Lent. For example, "Alleluia" is not used in worship during Lent – so be careful if you are choosing hymns, and if in doubt ask!

Easter Day
Liturgical colours: white or gold
Date: a Sunday between 22 March and 25 April

This is a time of rejoicing and celebrating Christ's resurrection from the dead. It is about the triumph of good over evil, life over death. The mood is very different – and "Alleluia" is again sung and said. Easter Day leads into Eastertide (Paschaltide), which lasts for fifty days.

Pentecost
Liturgical colour: red
Date: fiftieth day after Easter Day

This is another amazing event, when Christians focus on the descent of the Holy Spirit on the Apostles (Acts 2:1-12). Red symbolises fire and the Holy Spirit. You may hear Pentecost referred to as Whitsunday, or the birthday of the Church.

Holy days of obligation and other celebrations

The list above outlines the main seasons, feast days, festivals and solemnities which you will come across in the life of the school. You may also hear talk of holy days of obligation. These are days on which the faithful are obliged to participate in the Mass and to abstain from anything which prevents them from worshipping God. Every Sunday is a holy day of obligation, and some of the other days (such as the feast of the Epiphany on 6 January) are often celebrated on the nearest Sunday. So most of them will not be observed during school time. Occasionally, however, one will, and a Mass will be held at school. In addition, the school will have its own celebrations – such as observing its saint's day – and there may be other local celebrations.

The holy days of obligation are:

- The Nativity of the Lord (Christmas): 25 December.
- The Epiphany of the Lord: 6 January (in England, Wales and Scotland, transferred to the second Sunday after Christmas).
- The Ascension of the Lord: Thursday of the sixth week of Easter (in England and Wales, transferred to the following Sunday).
- The Most Holy Body and Blood of Christ (also known as Corpus Christi): Thursday after Trinity Sunday (in England, Wales and Scotland, transferred to the following Sunday).
- Saints Peter and Paul, Apostles: 29 June.*
- The Assumption of the Blessed Virgin Mary: 15 August.*
- All Saints: 1 November.*

* In England & Wales if it falls on a Saturday or Monday it is kept on the Sunday.

Liturgical colours

These will be used in the sanctuary decoration and the priest's vestments to reflect the mood of the season. White, red, green, purple and gold are the most common you will see, but black, blue and pink

are also used. If you see red, for example, at a time other than Pentecost, it generally means that a martyr or apostle is being commemorated on that day. Similarly, the third Sunday of Advent is known as "Gaudete" (rejoice) Sunday, when the penitential purple gives way to rose, or pink (Similarly, the fourth Sunday of Lent, which is Mothering Sunday). This explains why you will see three purple candles and one pink candle around the Advent wreath, with a white candle in the middle.

The sacraments

A sacrament is defined as an outward sign of inward grace – the action of God working within someone. The word comes from the Latin *sacramentum*, and came into use in the Church via the Roman army. A recruit became a soldier by taking an oath and being branded! As an initiated soldier, he then had responsibilities, and perks to go with them. This double status provided theologians with the model for what they were trying to illustrate when describing the rites of the Church as both spiritual and physical. The person receiving the sacrament simultaneously assumes new responsibilities and a new spiritual status before God. Happily the practice of branding was never used by the Church!

In the Catholic tradition there are seven sacraments. The first three – baptism, confirmation and Eucharist – are called the "sacraments of initiation", because they are all about entering the Christian community:

- **Baptism** is where someone (often as a baby) is admitted to the Church. The rite involves the use of prayer, the signing of the cross on the forehead, water, oil, light and a white garment.
- **Confirmation** is the sacrament that completes baptism; in it the gifts of the Holy Spirit are bestowed upon us.
- **The Eucharist, or Holy Communion, or Mass** is the sacrament in which Catholics receive the Body and Blood of Christ. It is seen as an act of unity with the whole Church. Catholics believe that, through a process of transubstantiation, Jesus becomes truly present in the Eucharistic bread (the host or Blessed Sacrament) and the Precious Blood. In the Catholic tradition it has become normal for someone to receive their First Holy Communion before confirmation. However, the ancient order of receiving confirmation first has been reintroduced into some dioceses.

The next two are called the "sacraments of healing":

- **Reconciliation** is sometimes called *confession* or *penance*, and is when a person confesses their sins and is forgiven. Catholics are asked to go to confession at least once a year at or near Easter – hopefully more frequently.
- **The sacrament of the sick** is given when someone is seriously ill or near death. Formerly this was referred to as the *Last Rites* or *Extreme Unction*.

Then there are the "sacraments of service and community":

- **Matrimony** (marriage).
- **Holy Orders** is the ordination of bishops, priests and deacons.

Am I likely to take part in any of the sacraments?
The school is an integral part of the faith community, so when a student, member of staff, or sometimes even a parent takes part in one of the sacraments it's not uncommon to invite teachers or staff members. It is a wonderful testament to the all-embracing nature of the Catholic faith and a demonstration of how life, faith and education are intertwined. In particular, First Holy Communion and reconciliation are very big events in the primary school calendar. Usually Year 3 pupils spend a lot of time preparing for them. Most of the preparation takes place in the parish and the home, although schools play an important supporting role. Schools often organise reconciliation during Advent or Lent, although some organise it more frequently. This might take the form of a priest visiting to hear individual confessions, or a larger penitential service, where several priests will be invited to hear confessions as part of a service.
(See Appendix II for how to prepare for this.)

Some primary school children celebrate First Holy Communion and first confession (reconciliation) and confirmation in Year 3, while others leave confirmation until Year 9 or 10. Either way, confirmation is another really big occasion. Preparation is done in the home and the parish, but again the school will be involved. Many teachers like to attend their students' confirmations.

Will I have to organise any of these celebrations?
If you work in a teaching role in a primary school it is highly likely that you will. In a secondary school, senior management or the chaplain will usually make arrangements. However, if you are the form tutor or teaching assistant, it is good to be part of the preparation. The most likely celebration you may be asked to help with is a class or school Mass, which may be held on a holy day of obligation or the school's saint's day or at the beginning and end of term. There should be plenty of advice and help available, and in Appendix II you will find a useful checklist for preparing for Mass or confession, along with an outline of what happens during Mass.

Daily worship and prayer

There is a statutory obligation for the school to hold a collective act of worship each day. For a Catholic school this can be as a whole school, a tutor group or a year group.

As a member of staff you are expected to support the school's prayer life. You may be attached to a class or a tutor group, in which case you will be asked to lead prayer or help pupils do so. If you are not part of any faith group, or if you are part of a non-Christian group, this can appear daunting, but there will always be plenty of support and advice available. Your task is to create opportunities for people to pray, if they choose to.

POINTS TO REMEMBER

- Everyone is included in the prayer life of the school.
- Everyone is on a learning curve in their understanding of the liturgy and the sacraments. If in doubt, ask for help.
- The liturgical seasons are excellent times for focusing and refocusing us on what matters – and are cause for celebration!
- The sacraments deepen our relationship with God and one another.
- Don't be afraid to express yourself within the liturgy. If you have an idea for developing the prayer life of the school, check with someone that it is acceptable – then go for it!
- If you are invited to a baptism, confirmation, etc., seriously consider going, and treat it as an opportunity to celebrate and learn.

POINTS FOR PERSONAL REFLECTION OR GROUP DISCUSSION

- How does your school celebrate the liturgical year?
- What would help you to develop your understanding of the sacraments and their importance?
- How do you feel about leading pupils in prayer? Would you like more training and help? If so, who might you approach?

People pray together, or as individuals, and prayers can be said inwardly or recited aloud. They may be spontaneous, or follow a written form. The Church is rich with a variety of ways of praying, including:

- Adoration: worshipping and adoring God.
- Confession: acknowledging wrongdoing and failings and asking for forgiveness.
- Intercession: praying on behalf of others or ourselves. This is sometimes called petitionary prayer (bidding prayers fall into this category).
- Praise: similar to adoration, but encompassing God's creation.
- Thanksgiving: offering thanks to God.

Appendix II has guidelines for prayer and worship with children and young people.

Reflection

SPOONFACE STEINBERG

Spoonface is a seven-year-old autistic Jewish girl dying of cancer. Spoonface tells us about a book that her doctor gave her to read from which she learnt about religion, praying, and how to make the most of life. The book tells her that in Poland:

When you smile, that is a prayer, when you talk, when you walk, and when you pray, when you spit, when you suck, when you snore... when the world was made God made it out of magic sparks and now the sparks are deep down inside, and the whole point of living is to find the spark. And when you see someone who is sad or injured or beaten up, all these people... all they need is help to find the spark... And there would be prayers for all the poor people with cancer. If only they could see the sparks...

AFTERWORD

Thinking about applying for a job in a Catholic school?

Should I apply?

Some people are put off applying for a job in a school when they see the word "Catholic". This might be because they object in principle to Catholic or faith schools, and it makes sense that they wouldn't feel comfortable in the job. For others, it's because they think that only Catholics can apply, or you have to be "holy" to do the job. But that's not the case. As we saw in Chapter 7, for the reserved posts (headteacher, deputy head, head of RE and RE co-ordinator) a practising commitment to the Catholic faith is required. For all other posts, the person specification usually stipulates "support for" or "sympathy with" the school's Catholic ethos (see Chapter 4). There is a further requirement in your contract that you will be required to "maintain the Catholic character of the school" and be conscious of and loyal to the aims and objectives of the school. But that is along the lines of what would be required in any school.

Simply the best

The desire among governors and headteachers is to appoint the best person for the job, who is willing to contribute to the Catholic life of the school. The students deserve the very best support and teaching. As we saw in Chapter 3, the Church is very clear about the high standards it expects in its schools. This means not only great teaching and exam results, but enrichment and support in their spiritual life.

Be yourself

So you've decided you want to give it a go! What next? Well, it's really very similar to any other application. The first thing is to get to know the school – have a look at the website and read the mission statement, the Ofsted reports, the results, any comments from agencies like the diocese or the local community, and then decide if you feel "called" to work there. The top tip for the application is "be yourself" – you don't have to pretend you're someone you're not. The selection panel will welcome honesty. From the outset, be clear about why you want this job and what you will bring to your role that will make a difference.

Getting to know you

During the interview stage, remember that it is as much about you getting a feel for the school and deciding whether you will be comfortable in the job, as the school choosing the best candidate. In other words, it should be a two-way process. There is no harm in asking to look around in advance of the interview, and you should certainly be offered a tour on the day itself. If at any point you decide it's not for you then you can withdraw. Again, it's better to be honest. If you are truthful and tactful, it should be respected and honoured.

Where do you see yourself in five years?

Most interview panels will ask how you would support the mission statement and Catholic ethos of the school, so it's worth having a few thoughts ready. You really don't need to blind anyone with theological insight – again, be yourself and show some understanding of what the school stands for. The best response might be to focus on what is unique about a Catholic school (see Chapter 3) – relationships and valuing the individual for who they are.

They often ask where you see yourself in five years' time. Again, there's no need to say what you think they want to hear. On one level it's a nonsense question. None of us knows what will happen tomorrow, never mind five years from now. There is a saying: "If you want to make God laugh, tell him your plans." However, it might give you a chance to give the panel some sense of your ambition and commitment.

Welcome to the family

Let's say you get the job – well done! This means they want you in the school and you have the confidence of the head and governors that you will do a great job. You will prepare for your new job as you would for any other. When you start there should be an induction programme when you will be able to explore working in a Catholic school in more depth. Just be open to what the school has to offer and enjoy making a difference to the lives of young people. No matter what your role is, you are teaching them in some way. It is one of the best things you could do with your life.

Pastoral care of staff

In a Catholic school much time and energy goes on supporting, educating and forming students. However, what many don't realise is that the governors, as well as your head and line manager, also have a serious duty of care for you as a professional and a person. Throughout *How to Survive Working in a Catholic School*, we have stressed the importance of the individual as a child of God. Adults are also God's children, just bigger and hopefully wiser! Although there is a plethora of policy documents and guidelines in every school, your spiritual welfare, happiness and well-being are equally important. Your line manager as well as the headteacher need to hear from you when you need support, so don't be afraid to say. Many Catholic state schools now devote one of their five INSET (professional development) days to spirituality, or looking together at the mission of the school. It is so important, with all the challenges we face and the pace at which we are expected to rise to those challenges, that we are given time to refresh ourselves and our sense of mission as a Catholic community.

APPENDIX 1

How to address the clergy and people in religious orders

This is a "how to" guide for introducing, addressing and corresponding with most of the clergy in the Catholic Church. For a "who's who" guide, see Chapter 7.

Addressing the pope

During a formal introduction the pope should be introduced as: "His Holiness the Pope"
He should be directly addressed as: "Your Holiness", or: "Holy Father"

On an envelope: "His Holiness Pope [Name, Number]", or: "His Holiness the Pope"
At the beginning of a letter: "Your Holiness", or: "Most Holy Father"

Addressing a cardinal

During a formal introduction, either: "His Eminence Cardinal [First Name, Surname], Archbishop of [Location]", or: "His Eminence Cardinal [First Name, Surname]". NB Which of these is correct depends whether or not the cardinal has a see (the domain of authority of a bishop). It's best to ask someone beforehand!
He should be directly addressed as: "Your Eminence", or: "Cardinal [Surname]"

On an envelope: "His Eminence Cardinal [First Name, Surname], Archbishop of [Location]"
At the beginning of a letter: "Your Eminence", or: "Dear Cardinal [Surname]"

Addressing an archbishop

During a formal introduction: "His Grace the Archbishop of [Location]"
He should be directly addressed as: "Your Grace", or: "Archbishop [Surname]"

On an envelope: "His Grace the Archbishop of [Location]", or: "The Most Reverend [First Name, Surname], Archbishop of [Location]"
At the beginning of a letter: "Your Grace", or: "Dear Archbishop [Surname]"

Addressing a bishop

During a formal introduction, a bishop should be introduced as: "His Lordship the Bishop of [Location]"
He should be directly addressed as: "My Lord", or: "Bishop [Surname]"

On an envelope: "The Right Reverend [First Name, Surname], Bishop of [Location]"
At the beginning of a letter: "Dear Bishop [Surname]"

Addressing a vicar general

During a formal introduction, a vicar general should be introduced as: "The Reverend Monsignor [First Name, Surname]"
He should be directly addressed as: "Monsignor [Surname]", or simply: "Monsignor"

On an envelope: "The Reverend Monsignor [First Name, Surname], VG"
At the beginning of a letter: "Dear Monsignor [Surname]"

Addressing a canon

During a formal introduction: "Canon [Surname]"
He should be directly addressed as: "Canon"

On an envelope: "The Reverend Canon [First Name, Surname]"
At the beginning of a letter: "Dear Canon [Surname]"

Addressing a priest

During a formal introduction: "The Reverend Father [First Name, Surname]"
He should be directly addressed as: "Father [Surname]", or simply: "Father"

On an envelope: "The Reverend Father [First Name, Surname]"
At the beginning of a letter: "Dear Father [Surname]"

Addressing a priest who is a member of a religious congregation or order

During a formal introduction: "The Reverend Father [First Name, Surname] of the [Name of his Religious Order (e.g., Society of Jesus)]"
He should be directly addressed as: "Father [Surname]", or simply: "Father"

On an envelope: "The Reverend Father [First Name, Surname, Initials of his Religious Order (e.g., SJ)]"
At the beginning of a letter: "Dear Father [Surname]"

Addressing a deacon

During a formal introduction: "The Reverend Deacon [First Name, Surname]"
He should be directly addressed as: "Deacon [Last Name]"

On an envelope: "The Reverend Deacon [First Name, Surname]"
At the beginning of a letter: "Dear Deacon [Surname]"

Addressing a lay chaplain

Simply use their formal name in public and follow the rules of the school for the protocols for addressing staff.

Addressing a religious brother

During a formal introduction: "Brother [First Name (and Surname, if known)] of the [Name of his Religious Order (e.g., Order of Friars Minor)]"
He should be directly addressed as: "Brother [First Name]"

On an envelope: "Brother [First Name (and Surname, if known), Initials of Religious Order (e.g., OFM)]"
At the beginning of a letter: "Dear Brother [First Name]"

Addressing a religious sister

During a formal introduction: "Sister [First Name (and Surname, if known)] of the [Name of her Religious Order (e.g., Daughters of St Paul)]"
She should be directly addressed as: "Sister [First Name]", or: "Sister"

On an envelope: "Sister [First Name, Surname, Initials of her Religious Order (e.g., DSP)]"
At the beginning of a letter: "Dear Sister [First Name]"

APPENDIX II

A checklist for preparing for a religious service or prayers

Before the day, make sure you have arranged that the priest be present and you have discussed the celebration with him. It is very helpful to have everything written out for him.
Some things to consider are:

- Who will be taking part? Which priest will be celebrating? Which class? Are other staff involved? Does everyone know who and what is involved?
- When and where is the celebration to be held? Make sure everyone knows.
- What scripture readings and Bible translation are you using? Check that the priest is happy with your choice, and be aware that the readings for certain days should not be changed.
- How are you going to prepare the room? Flowers and artwork reflecting the theme are helpful but be aware that flowers should not be used during Lent.
- Are you going to have music? If so, check who is leading and choosing the music. Be careful, as there are rules about what may and may not be sung in the different seasons. Check with the head of RE or RE co-ordinator.

Vestments for the priest

Most schools will have these. If not, ask the priest to bring his own. Remember that they are colour coded according to the season or feast. The basics are an *alb* (a plain white tunic), a *stole* (which the priest wears around his neck) and a *chasuble* (an outer garment).

Bible translations

The Bible is the word of God and must always be handled with great respect. There are many different Bible translations, ranging from the *King James Bible* in old English, to more modern versions such as the *New Revised Standard Version* and the *Jerusalem Bible* (the translation used in the Catholic Lectionary). Your RE co-ordinator or head of RE will guide you as to which is best.

The furniture

- **Altar:** the table of the Lord, around which the people gather to celebrate the sacrifice of the Mass.
- **Altar cloth:** there should be at least one white cloth covering the altar.
- **Altar crucifix:** you need a crucifix on or close to the altar.
- **Bell:** the server rings the bell as the priest shows the host and then the chalice.
- **Bowl or jug:** a bowl or jug of water and towel are used for the priest symbolically to purify his hands before consecrating the bread and wine.
- **Chair:** a chair for the priest

- **Candles:** used at every liturgical celebration to represent Christ the light of the world.
- **Chalice:** the cup that holds the Blood of Christ.
- **Corporal:** an additional smaller cloth is placed at the centre of the altar for the paten and chalice to be placed on.
- **Credence table:** a small side table on which rests the sacred vessels.
- **Cruets:** small jugs or bottles, one holding water and one wine.
- **Flowers:** the use of flowers is optional, although no flowers are used in Lent.
- **Lectern:** the stand which holds the lectionary.
- **Lectionary:** a book containing the scripture readings.
- **Paten:** a plate used to hold the altar bread for Communion.
- **Place to reserve the unconsumed hosts.**
- **Purificator:** used to wipe the lip of the chalice between one person taking Communion and the next, as well as cleaning the sacred vessels after Mass.
- **Roman Missal:** a large book containing the prayers for the celebration of Mass.

The cross

A cross will be needed as a focal point for any service you are preparing. You will see many different crosses around the school, and each design generally has a particular symbolism. Try to select the right type for the age group. Sometimes a more unusual cross is very effective because, as with all signs and symbols, over-familiarity can diminish significance.

The structure of the Mass

The following is a chronological outline of what happens during Mass. There are antiphons, hymns and prayers throughout:

- **Gathering the community for the celebration:** everyone comes to the location in a reverent manner. Music/singing is a great way to begin.
- **Welcome:** by the priest.
- **Penitential Act:** this is where the community expresses sorrow for anything that has separated them from God and/or one another. It can be sung.
- **Gloria:** this is used on holy days of obligation or other special occasions – but not on ordinary days or Sundays in Advent or Lent. It should be sung if music is being used.
- **Collect of the Mass:** a set prayer for the day, said by the priest.
- **Liturgy of the Word:** everything in the Mass up to and including the Prayer of the Faithful (see below). This part of the service includes the readings and psalm. There are set readings for each day, but unless it is a holy day of obligation, a solemnity or a feast, the readings may be specifically chosen. Make sure the priest is happy with your choice. Pupils or members of staff can do these readings but not the Gospel.
- **Alleluia or Gospel acclamation:** Alleluia is not used in Lent, although a Gospel acclamation is.
- **Gospel:** this is a reading from one of the four Gospels in the New Testament (Matthew, Mark, Luke and John). The priest or deacon will read this.
- **Homily:** the priest will give a short talk on the meaning of the readings.
- **The Creed:** this is the prayer that expresses the community's faith. It is recited only on Sundays and Solemnities.

- **Prayer of the Faithful:** sometimes called "bidding prayers". Here the pupils or staff can read prayers for the Church and community.
- **Liturgy of the Eucharist:** this describes the next stage of the Mass, in which the priest and people turn their attention to the sacrament itself – the Eucharist.
- **The presentation of the gifts (bread and wine):** the procession of offerings (bread and wine for consecration, the collection plate or other symbolic offerings) to the altar. This is done by staff and pupils.
- **The Eucharistic Prayer:** during this the Holy, Holy and the Acclamation should be sung.
- **The Our Father:** also known as the Lord's Prayer, this is the prayer that Jesus taught (see Matthew 6:9-13 and Luke 11:2-4).
- **The sign of peace:** here we turn to one another and shake hands.
- **The Lamb of God:** also known as the Agnus Dei, this is sung or recited while the priest breaks the host.
- **Communion:** those who have already made their first Communion and are still practising, are invited to go forward to receive Holy Communion from the priest or Minister of Communion. People who are not Catholic or not going to receive Communion may go up for a blessing. Here they simply cross their arms over their chest to indicate that they are coming for a blessing. It is good to sing a hymn during this time or play a reflective piece of music.
- **Concluding Rites:** the community is blessed and sent forth.

Preparing for individual confession

The school will have a suitable room or area that can be used for individual confession. This needs to be carefully arranged with safeguarding requirements in mind. Although the pupil is going to see the priest alone, they are kept in sight (but not earshot) at all times, to safeguard both parties. Having made their confession, there should be a quiet area where the pupils can pray. Quiet music can create a reflective atmosphere.

Whatever someone says in confession is strictly confidential. However, it is worth understanding the seal of confession and how it differs from confidentiality.

Preparing for a penitential service

The community gathers around a suitable focal point. The structure of the service will be:

- an opening hymn
- opening prayers
- scripture readings
- the homily
- examination of conscience
- Litany
- individual confession (people will go one at a time to a priest sitting to the side)
- blessing and dismissal

Guidelines for prayer and worship with children and young people

Remember, keep it:

- God-centred
- God-led
- relevant
- in the right mood
- related to the season
- employing the senses

Less is best – remember that silence works, and leave space for God.

Things used for prayer:

- stations of the cross
- prayer walks
- prayer gardens
- liturgical banners
- rosary
- scripture
- sacred space
- prayer corner/tables
- prayer books
- medals
- adoration of the Blessed Sacrament

Developing prayer

Just like every other learning area, prayer needs to be taught in a systematic and relevant way. What is appropriate with one group may not work with another. Following is a suggestion for a year-by-year introduction – each stage building on the previous one. If you need the words for any of the prayers, senior management or the chaplain will be able to supply them.

- **Step 1:** create a sacred space and prayer focal point. Introduce prayer as a quiet time for talking and listening to God. Teach the children to make the sign of the cross. Use a holy water font, and teach prayer using the symbolism of water (cleansing, purifying, etc.). Introduce the idea of talking to God for a few moments several times a day.
- **Step 2:** prepare the children to talk and listen to Jesus. Use music and light. Develop the meaning of the sign of the cross (the special sign which shows I am a Christian). Explain the use of holy water and why the act of blessing is important. Teach the Hail Mary, Our Father and school prayer. Talk about why we pray at mealtimes, and introduce the idea of spontaneous prayers for different occasions – happy occasions, sorrow, gratitude, prayers when you need help, etc.
- **Step 3:** encourage each child to make a personal prayer journal in which they record their thoughts and prayers, pictures, etc. These can be used each day, taking turns to share prayers from them. Discuss how someone can pray at any time as well as set times. As a group, write prayers for different seasons. Look at the words and their meaning in the Our Father and Hail Mary. Learn about blessing prayers for different occasions and acts of sorrow.
- **Step 4:** start to spend longer in prayer. Use scripture verses and accounts as a stimulus for prayer and start to think about using imagination in prayer. Think about a character (for example, from the Gospels) speaking to Jesus, listening to him and learning from him. Teach the Glory Be prayer.
- **Step 5:** think about prayer in our hearts and learning to be still and quiet, reflective and meditative. Use music such as Taizé or Gregorian chant to aid prayer and reflection.
- **Step 6:** teach about traditional methods of prayer, and adapt them to the pupils' needs. Pupils make their own special prayer bracelets, crosses and beads. Start to see prayer as the "air we breathe". Talk about praying frequently and spontaneously.
- **Step 7:** use images, symbols and sounds in prayer – water, light, objects, music, artwork, etc. Discuss seeing God in all creation, especially nature.
- **Step 8:** start to think about prayer as an offering of our lives. Teach the Morning Offering prayer, and invite pupils to compose their own version. Introduce the Prayer of the Church, and adapt a simple version.

Ideas for a daily act of worship and prayer

The possibilities are endless, but here are some simple prayer ideas for using with a class:

- **The register:** a simple way of inviting each child in turn to be responsible for the day's prayer focus. Each day invite one person to say what they would like the class to pray for. The name and focus then go on the board for the day.

- **The news:** the teacher can select an appropriate item for prayer for younger pupils. For Year 2 upwards they can choose for themselves. (Either way, this should be thought about the day before.)
- **Objects:** pupils might bring something in, or the teacher may select an appropriate item.
- **Candles:** a candle can be passed from person to person and they can either pray silently or out loud for their intention. This can also be used to think about a common theme, e.g., "I will be a light to the world today by..."
- **A line from scripture:** depending on the age group, allow pupils to select a scripture card that says, for example, "Love one another... as I have loved you", or "I am the light of the world". Allow each child to pick a card that speaks to them and quietly think about it. This can be in silence, or shared reflection time.
- **Items that reflect scripture messages:** choose a suitable rock, stone or brick. How are we these things for one another?
- **Water:** can be used to signify blessings or a renewal of commitment to the class charter or promises. Each person dips their finger in a bowl of water blessed by a priest and makes the sign of the cross and silently prays for their intention.
- **Praying for different countries:** using a world map and coloured flags, place a pin on the country you wish to pray for. This can be a single focus prayer or invite each person to choose a country. Say why they want to pray for that country.
- **Name prayers:** each child uses their name as an acrostic prayer. This can be used in conjunction with the register prayer.
- **Incense:** each person takes a grain of incense and names someone or something they wish to pray for. Then they place it on lit charcoal in a fireproof container. When it is lit, the incense symbolises our prayers rising to God.
- **Music meditation:** music is excellent for helping children to meditate without words. Begin by introducing the theme with as few words as possible and then allow the music to take them into prayer.
- **Hands, feet, eyes, ears, mouth:** start with the St Teresa of Avila prayer (see page 56). How are they going to use their hands, etc., to continue Christ's work?
- **Prayer journals:** this is an excellent way of encouraging people to develop a personal prayer life. (For ideas on how to use them, see the "Developing prayer" section above.)
- **Cards:** invite the children to bring in a Christmas or birthday card as a focus, either for praying for the person who sent it, or using the picture as a meditation, e.g., thinking about the magi (wise men) near the feast of Epiphany.
- **A prayer garden:** this can be a class, year group or whole school project. Select an area in the school grounds and invite the pupils to design a garden as a place for prayer and reflection. Invite each family to provide some small thing to go into the garden. Set up a working team to build and maintain the garden.
- **Prayer stations:** station simply means "waiting place". Create little areas – waiting places with a focus for prayer around the school – either as permanent features or as a temporary exercise. They can be thematic, scriptural, seasonal, or cover a wide range of possibilities. You could invite the children and their families to design a station.

A GLOSSARY OF CATHOLIC TERMS

The following list is by no means exhaustive, but it includes many words and phrases you may well come across.

A

Absolution: Part of the sacrament of reconciliation. It is the formal declaration by the priest that a penitent's sins are forgiven.

Abstinence: Refraining from certain kinds of food or drink as an act of self-denial. Official days when Catholics abstain from eating meat are Ash Wednesday and Good Friday; in 2011 the bishops of England and Wales called upon Catholics to re-establish the practice on other Fridays throughout the year (and on CAFOD fast days), to mark the day on which Jesus died.

Advent: The season of the Church's year leading up to Christmas. It includes the four Sundays before Christmas and it is a time of preparation for the coming of Christ. Advent marks the beginning of the Church's year.

All Saints' Day: The day on which Catholics remember all the saints of the Church, whether officially canonised or not. It is celebrated on 1 November.

All Souls' Day: The day on which Catholics remember the dead and pray for them, recognising those that may still need to be brought to perfection. It is observed on 2 November.

Altar: The table of the Lord, around which the people gather to celebrate the sacrifice of the Mass.

Angel: The word means "messenger". In the Bible they are described as carrying messages from God to human beings.

Angelus: A form of prayer said three times a day: in the morning, at noon and in the evening. When said in monasteries or churches it is customary to ring the bells.

Annunciation: The "announcement" by the angel Gabriel to Mary that she was to be the mother of the Saviour. The feast of the Annunciation is celebrated on 25 March.

Apostolate: The work of an apostle. It is used to describe any work, ministry or service which is carried out on behalf of the Church. For example, the apostolate of a religious order is the work the order undertakes.

Ascension: The taking up of Jesus into heaven forty days after the resurrection and witnessed by the apostles. Ascension Day is celebrated forty days after Easter or on the following Sunday.

Ash Wednesday: The first day of Lent. By tradition Catholics have ashes put on their foreheads or heads on this day as a mark of repentance. They also fast on this day and abstain from eating meat.

Assumption: The taking up of Mary the mother of Jesus into heaven. Catholics celebrate this on 15 August.

Ave Maria: Latin words meaning "Hail Mary", the first words of the most popular prayer Catholics address to Mary.

B

Basilica: A large and significant church. The most famous is St Peter's Basilica in Rome.

Beatification: The first step in the process by which a dead person is officially declared to be a saint.

Benediction: A service in which the consecrated host is placed in a monstrance (see p. 86) where it can be seen and venerated by the people. At the conclusion of the service the priest blesses the people with the monstrance containing the host.

Bidding prayers: Prayers which are said at Mass for the needs of the Church and the world. Also referred to as "the prayer of the faithful". (For more about prayer, see Chapter 8.)

Blessed Sacrament: A term Catholics use when referring to the consecrated host – especially when it is reserved in the tabernacle (see p. 88).

Blessing: A short prayer, usually accompanied by the sign of the cross, asking God's favour on persons or objects.

Breviary: A book containing the prayers, hymns, psalms and readings which make up the Divine Office – the official prayer of the Church said at various times during the day.

C

Canonisation: The official declaration by the pope that a dead person is a saint and may be publicly venerated.

Canon Law: The law of the Church.

Catechism: A written summary of Christian teaching.

Catechist: Someone who teaches Christian doctrine, especially in parish or school.

Celebrant: The one who presides at a religious service. The priest at Mass is referred to as the celebrant.

Chalice: The cup used at Mass to hold the wine (precious blood).

Chapter: The governing body of a cathedral or other religious community.

Chrism: A mixture of olive oil and balsam which is blessed by the bishop in Holy Week and is used in the administration of the sacraments of baptism, confirmation and holy orders, and in the consecration of altars.

Christmas: The feast of the birth of Jesus, celebrated on 25 December.

Christ the King: Now known as "Our Lord Jesus Christ, King of the Universe", this feast is celebrated on the last Sunday of the Church's year acclaiming Christ as king of the universe.

Ciborium: A bowl or chalice-shaped vessel to hold the consecrated hosts for the distribution of Holy Communion.

Clergy: A term applied to men who have been ordained for ministry within the Church. Bishops, priests and deacons are members of the clergy.

Communion under both kinds: Receiving Holy Communion under both the forms of bread and wine. It is becoming increasingly common for Catholics to receive Holy Communion in this way, particularly on special occasions.

Concelebration: The celebration of Mass by several priests together.

Conclave: The meeting of the cardinals, in complete seclusion, when they assemble to elect a pope.

Confessor: A priest who hears confessions.

Consecration: Making something sacred. It describes the moment during Mass when God changes the bread and wine into the Body and Blood of Christ.

Contrition: The acknowledgement of sin and sorrow for it.

Convent: The place where a community of nuns lives.

Corpus Christi: A Latin phrase meaning "the Body of Christ". The feast of Corpus Christi commemorates the institution of the Eucharist and is celebrated on the Thursday after Trinity Sunday.

Creed: A summary of Christian beliefs.

Crucifix: A cross with the figure of the crucified Jesus upon it. Used by Catholics to bring to mind the sufferings, kingship and triumph of Christ.

CWL: Stands for Catholic Women's League: an organisation which promotes religious education and social welfare and represents Catholic women's interests on national and international bodies.

D

Deanery: Several parishes form a deanery, sometimes called a "pastoral area". This unit is administered by one of the priests of the deanery who has the title "Dean".

Devil: The name for the evil one, a creature who rebelled against God and causes evil.

Diocese: An area under the care of a bishop.

Dispensation: Exemption from a church law in a particular case for a special reason.

Doctrines: The beliefs of Catholics, expressed in the Creed and other official documents.

Dogma: Doctrines put forward by the Church which are to be accepted as true and clear statements of belief.

E

Easter: The day on which Jesus rose.

Ecumenism: The work for unity between the different Christian Churches.

Enclosure: That part of a convent or monastery to which outsiders are not admitted.

Encyclical: A letter from the pope to the whole Church, usually dealing with matters of faith and the Christian life.

Epiphany: The feast which commemorates the visit of the magi to the infant Christ in Bethlehem. It is celebrated on 6 January or on the second Sunday after Christmas.

Excommunication: Cutting someone off from the community of the Church because of serious offences against its law or teaching. It is resorted to only rarely.

F

Fasting: Eating less food than usual as an act of self-denial. Catholics fast especially on Ash Wednesday and Good Friday.

Feast day: A day of special solemnity within the Church.

First Friday: See "Sacred Heart".

Font: A basin or bowl in a church used for the baptismal water.

Friday penance: In commemoration of the sufferings of Christ, Catholics perform some act of self-denial every Friday. This may take the form of abstaining from meat, or some other food, or doing an act of charity.

G

Genuflection: Kneeling on one knee as a sign of honour and worship to Jesus Christ and an expression of faith in his presence in the tabernacle under the form of bread. Catholics genuflect when entering and leaving a church.

Godparent: Someone who assists the parents in ensuring that a child who is baptised will be brought up in the Catholic faith. The godparent must be a Catholic, though he or she may be assisted by a witness who is a member of another Christian Church.

Good Friday: The day on which the crucifixion of Jesus is commemorated. It is a day of special solemnity for Catholics. They fast and abstain from meat on this day.

Gospel: A word meaning "Good News". The proclamation of the good news of salvation won for us by Jesus Christ. The word is also used of the four books which tell of the life, death and resurrection of Jesus: the Gospels of Matthew, Mark, Luke and John.

Grace: The gift of God's love and help which is given to us freely, without any previous efforts on our part.

Grace at meals: A short prayer before and after meals thanking God for the food we eat and asking his blessing on those who have prepared it.

H

Habit: The distinctive form of dress worn by members of religious communities.

Hail Mary: The most popular prayer Catholics address to Our Lady (see p. 86). It derives from the angel's greeting (Luke 1:28) and the greeting of Mary's cousin Elizabeth (Luke 1:42), adding to these a request to Mary to pray for us. The full prayer is: "Hail Mary, full of grace, the Lord is with thee; blessed art thou amongst women and blessed is the fruit of thy womb, Jesus. Holy Mary, Mother of God, pray for us sinners now and at the hour of our death. Amen."

Heaven: The endless moment of love. Nothing more separates us from God, whom our soul loves and has sought our whole life long.

Hell: The condition of everlasting separation from God which our freedom makes possible.

Heresy: A teaching that contradicts the beliefs of the Catholic Church.

Holy day of obligation: A solemnity – when the faithful are obliged to participate in the Mass, and to abstain from anything which prevents them from worshipping God. Every Sunday is a holy day of obligation (see Chapter 8).

Holy Hour: A service in which Jesus is venerated in the Blessed Sacrament.

Holy Saturday: The day between Good Friday and Easter Sunday.

Holy Thursday (or Maundy Thursday): The day before Good Friday. On this day Catholics commemorate the supper Jesus had with his disciples on the night before he died.

Holy water: Water that has been blessed by a priest. Catholics bless themselves with holy water as they make the sign of the cross on entering a church as a reminder of their baptism. Holy water is used for various blessings and at home.

Holy Week: The final week of Lent, leading up to Easter Sunday. The last three days of Holy Week (Holy Thursday, Good Friday and Holy Saturday) are days of special solemnity.

Homily: see "Sermon".

Host: The consecrated Eucharist in the form of bread; the large host is broken by the priest at Mass, and small hosts are used to distribute to the people, and to reserve in the Tabernacle. Also used casually to mean unconsecrated altar-breads.

I

Icon: Prayed depiction of Christ, Mary, or the saints painted in the style of the Eastern (Orthodox) Church. Often painted on wood and adorned with precious stones.

Immaculate Conception: The doctrine that Mary was conceived without inheriting original sin. (Not to be confused with the virgin birth of Jesus.)

Impediment to marriage: Something which prevents a person entering into a church marriage. For example, certain degrees of blood-relationship between the partners, or where one partner is not baptised. A dispensation can be obtained from some impediments.

Incarnation: The mystery of the wonderful union of the divine and human natures in the person of Jesus Christ.

Indulgence: Remission of the punishment or penance due to sin after its guilt has been forgiven.

Intercession: The prayers the saints in heaven offer to God on behalf of people on earth who request their help.

J

Jesus: There are a number of symbols for the name Jesus which you may see in churches or in works of religious art. These are some of them:

- *ICHTHYS*: an acrostic consisting of the initial letters of five Greek words forming the word for fish, which represent the divine character of Jesus: *Iesous* (Jesus), *Christos* (Christ), *Theou* (God's), *Yios* (Son), *Soter* (Saviour).
- *INRI*: the initial letters from the Latin inscription written on the cross: "Iesus Nazarenus Rex Iudaeorum" (Jesus of Nazareth, King of the Jews).
- *XP*: a monogram of the first two Greek letters of "Christos".

Joseph: The husband of Mary, venerated as a saint. His feast is celebrated on 19 March.

K

Kyrie, eleison: Greek words meaning "Lord, have mercy". Sometimes said or sung in Greek during the Penitential Act of the Mass.

L

Laity: Members of the Church who do not belong to the clergy or a religious order.

Last judgement: The judgement of every person by Jesus Christ at the end of time.

Last Supper: The supper Jesus had with his disciples on the night before he died, during which he instituted the Eucharist.

Lay apostolate: Work done by lay people as a response to their baptismal calling.

Lectern: The stand from which the scriptures are read in church.

Lectionary: The book containing the scripture readings for Mass and other celebrations.

Lent: A period of six weeks leading up to Easter. It begins on Ash Wednesday and is a time of self-denial in preparation for Easter. Catholics usually choose some form of self-denial which they observe during Lent.

Litany: A form of prayer in which the minister recites a series of petitions to God, or calls on the help of the saints. These petitions are followed by a set response said or sung by the congregation.

Liturgical year: The worship of the Church over the period of a year during which the central mysteries of faith are unfolded. The chief festivals are Christmas, Easter and Pentecost.

Liturgy: The public worship of the Church.

Lord's Prayer: The prayer Jesus taught his followers to say: the Our Father.

M

Magisterium: The teaching authority of the Church.

Martyr: A Christian who bears witness to the truth of the Gospel to the point of death.

Mass: Eucharist. (For more about the sacraments, see Chapter 8.)

Maundy Thursday: See "Holy Thursday".

May devotions: Special services held during the month of May to honour Mary, the mother of Jesus.

Meditation: Reflecting on God or the things of God in one's own heart.

Missal: A book containing the prayers of the Mass.

Missionaries: Christians who proclaim the Gospel to non-Christians in a foreign country. It is also often applied to anyone who endeavours to share his or her faith with others.

Mixed marriage: A marriage between a Catholic and a Christian of a different denomination. Catholics need permission from the Church before they can contract such a marriage.

Monstrance: An ornate (sometimes) receptacle in which a consecrated host is placed so that Jesus, in the form of bread, can be seen and venerated by the people.

Mortal sin: A serious sin by which a Christian cuts himself or herself off from God's grace. Catholics who are conscious of having committed a mortal sin are bound to confess to a priest.

Mother of God: A title given to Mary because she is the mother of Jesus who is both God and man.

Mystery: A truth which cannot be grasped by human reason.

N

New Testament: That part of the Bible which tells the Good News of Jesus Christ.

Novena: Nine days of prayer. It has its origin in the nine days the disciples spent in prayer awaiting the coming of the Holy Spirit, between the ascension and Pentecost.

Nuptial Mass: A Mass which includes the wedding service. Not all weddings in the Catholic Church are celebrated within Mass. It is quite common to have the wedding service alone.

O

Old Testament: That part of the Bible written before the time of Christ.

Ordination: The conferring of holy orders on a man, by which he becomes a bishop, priest or deacon.

Original sin: refers, not to personal sin, but rather to the fallen state of humankind into which the individual is born.

Our Lady: The title Catholics most frequently use when referring to Mary, the mother of Jesus.

P

Pagan: A collective term meaning "unbelievers".

Palm Sunday: The Sunday before Easter. It commemorates the occasion when Jesus rode into Jerusalem on a donkey and the people waved palm branches in his honour. In the Catholic Church this Sunday is now called Palm Sunday of the Passion of the Lord.

Parables: The stories Jesus told which illustrate some of his most important teachings.

Paradise: Another word for heaven. It is also used of the Garden of Eden.

Parish: The community of the Church in a particular place.

Parish council: A group of people of a parish who, together with the parish priest, look after various needs of the parish.

Parish mission: A period of spiritual renewal within a parish, usually conducted by one or more visiting priests over a period of a week or a fortnight.

Passion: The suffering and death of Jesus on the cross endured for our salvation.

Passion Sunday: See "Palm Sunday".

Pastoral care: The caring work of the Church, particularly that exercised by ordained ministers. "Pastor" means "shepherd".

Pastoral letter: A letter sent from a bishop to his diocese on a number of occasions during the year. Pastoral letters are usually read out to the people during the Mass.

Pax Christi: Literally "the peace of Christ". It is the name of an international Catholic movement for peace.

Penance: As well as referring to the sacrament of penance or reconciliation (see Chapter 8), the word "penance" also refers to acts of self-denial. For example, fasting can be described as an act of penance.

Pentecost: Literally means "fiftieth day". It marks the day when the Holy Spirit came upon the apostles fifty days after the resurrection of Jesus. Also called Whit Sunday.

Petition: Asking God for our needs in prayer.

Pilgrimage: A journey to a holy place. Popular places of pilgrimage today include the Holy Land, Rome, Walsingham and Lourdes.

Postulant: A person who has applied to join a religious order and is waiting to be admitted. Can also be called "candidate" or "aspirant".

Prayer of the Faithful: See "Bidding prayers".

Preaching: The proclamation of the Gospel, challenging the listener to make a commitment. "To preach" also means "to deliver a sermon".

Preface: The first part of the Eucharistic Prayer in the Mass.

Presbytery: The house, often adjoining the church, where the priest of the parish lives.

Procession: A solemn walk for a religious purpose, usually accompanied by prayers and hymns. Processions are not as common nowadays as they once were, but they are still held occasionally. For example, May processions in honour of Our Lady, or processions for Corpus Christi.

Profession: The taking of vows on joining a religious order.

Purgatory: A state in which the souls of the dead are purified and perfected in love before finally becoming one with God in heaven.

R

Readers: Those who read the scripture passages during Mass. Passages from the Old Testament or parts of the New Testament may be read by lay people (men and women). Passages from the Gospels are always read by a priest or deacon.

Real presence: The phrase Catholics use to indicate their belief that the bread and wine offered during the Mass become the Body and Blood of Christ.

Redemption: Being delivered from evil through the birth, life, death and resurrection of Jesus Christ.

Reformation: A movement for the reform of certain doctrines and practices of the Church which began in the sixteenth century and led to the division between Catholic and Protestant (or Reformed) Churches.

Religious order: Name given to communities of men or women dedicated to some specific mission. See "Vows".

Requiem: A Mass for the dead. It takes its name from the first word of the prayer with which the Mass begins. In Latin this is: "Requiem aeternam dona eis, Domine." (Lord, give them eternal rest.)

Responsorial psalm: A psalm which is recited or sung after the first scripture reading at Mass. The congregation recites or sings a response after each verse.

Resurrection of the body: The doctrine that at the end of time all will rise, body and soul, from the dead and live with God for ever or be condemned.

Revelation: God's disclosure of himself to humanity. The greatest revelation of God is Jesus Christ.

Rosary: A form of prayer reflecting on the main events in the life of Jesus and Mary, his mother. There are twenty of these events, called "mysteries", divided into four groups of five: Joyful, Luminous, Sorrowful and Glorious. The prayers which go with each mystery are: one Our Father; ten Hail Marys; one Glory be to the Father. Rosary beads are used to help count the prayers. The repetition of the prayer is an aid to concentration and is used in rather the same way that a mantra is used in some Eastern religions.

S

Sacrament: A rite or ceremony which imparts divine grace. In the Catholic Church there are seven sacraments: baptism, confirmation, the Eucharist, reconciliation (also known as penance), marriage, holy orders and anointing the sick (sometimes known as Extreme Unction or the Last Rites). (For more about the sacraments, see Chapter 8.)

Sacramentals: Rites, objects or actions intended to aid devotion which have some resemblance to sacraments but were not instituted by Christ. An example of a sacramental is the use of holy water.

Sacred Heart: The heart of Jesus is honoured as a sign of his love for all people. The feast of the Most Sacred Heart of Jesus is celebrated in June and there is a tradition among many Catholics of honouring Jesus under this title on the first Friday of every month.

Sacristy: The room in the church where the priest vests for Mass and other services and where the sacred vessels are kept.

Saints: Members of the Church whose holiness of life is recognised after their death and who are venerated by the Church on earth. Before anyone is proclaimed as a saint (canonised) a process of careful investigation of his or her life is carried out.

Sanctuary lamp: A lamp which is kept burning near the tabernacle in Catholic churches as a sign and a reminder that Jesus is present in the Blessed Sacrament.

Seminary: A college where men are trained for the priesthood.

Sign of the cross: A formula Catholics use to bless themselves. It is made with the right hand by touching the forehead, the breast and the shoulders while saying the words: "In the name of the Father, and of the Son and of the Holy Spirit. Amen." Catholics make the sign of the cross at the beginning of Mass, at the beginning of other forms of prayer, and sometimes when beginning an activity or at the start of a new day.

Sin: A rejection of God, usually through action or inaction.

Soul: The spiritual element of a person's nature.

Stations of the cross: A series of fourteen meditations on incidents from the suffering and death of Christ. Images of these fourteen scenes can be found round Catholic churches. There is sometimes a fifteenth one, "the resurrection".

SVP: Stands for "Society of St Vincent de Paul": a society of men and women willing to undertake active charitable works.

Synod: A church council, for example the synod of bishops which is held in Rome at roughly three-year intervals and is attended by about two hundred bishops from all over the world.

T

Tabernacle: Usually an ornate box where the Blessed Sacrament is reserved.

Ten Commandments: The rules of life delivered by God to Moses on Mount Sinai. They still form the basis of morality for Christians.

Theology: Articulating and exploring our experience of God, who reveals himself to us.

Tradition: The teaching which has been handed down from the apostles of Jesus and which continues to be handed on by the Church in every age.

Transubstantiation: A word Catholics use to describe the way in which Jesus becomes present in the Eucharistic bread and wine.

Trinity Sunday: The Sunday after Pentecost. A day on which even more special honour is paid to the Blessed Trinity.

U

UCM: Stands for "Union of Catholic Mothers", an organisation of Catholic married women for the preservation of faith and morals in the home.

V

Vatican: A sovereign city state and the official residence of the pope in Rome. It also refers to the central government of the Church.

Venial sin: A sin which is not so serious that it requires the sacrament of penance for its forgiveness.

Vestments: Garments worn by the ministers of the Church when celebrating Mass or administering the sacraments. These include the *alb* – a long white tunic worn by all ministers; the *chasuble* – the main outer garment of the priest when celebrating Mass; the *stole* – a type of scarf worn round the neck. The stole is worn by all clergy when administering the sacraments.

Viaticum: Holy Communion given to a person who is dying. The word means "provision for a journey", namely, the journey through death to life in the world to come.

Virgin birth: The doctrine that Mary remained a virgin both before, during and after the birth of Jesus, her son. This doctrine preserves the truth that Jesus was both God and man. He was "conceived by the Holy Spirit", meaning that his origin is wholly from God; he was "born of the Virgin Mary", meaning that he is fully human.

Vocation: The calling to a life of love, service and holiness which is addressed to all people. The word is also commonly used in a specific sense to refer to the calling to the priesthood or religious life.

Vows: Solemn promises of poverty, chastity and obedience which are made to God by members of religious orders. They can be temporary (binding only for a time) or perpetual (binding for life). Vows can also refer to those of marriage, baptism, etc.

W

Whitsunday: Another name for the feast of Pentecost which celebrates the coming of the Holy Spirit on the apostles. "Whit" means "white". In earlier times the newly baptised wore the white robes of baptism on this day.